Reach Your Full Potential!

Learn To:

- **Develop Confidence**

- **Establish Goals**

- **Improve Your Memory**

- **Practice Proven Study Strategies and Skills**

"Learn to be The Master Student is an invaluable tool for today's students. It makes the vital connection between self-esteem, study skills, and academic success. I recommend it highly."

Dr. Vincent Reed
Former Superintendent
District of Columbia Public Schools

Scholarship offer is on page 237.

For our readers:

We wanted to help with the quest for success,
So we wrote a few words for some to digest.
We've written a book for all students to see,
That there are no limits to what they desire to be.

As you looked at the cover, the book you can see,
The title of which is "Learn to be,
The Master Student," with a subtitle that shows,
How all of the students can get in the know.

We know there are skeptics, we hope just a few,
But we want them to think as champions do.
So they can learn what they must, and achieve far beyond,
Their dreams, the greatest, their desires most fond.

This book is geared for grades twelve to nine,
And college students, too, we hope that is fine.
There's something here for kids of all ages,
When parents help to go through the pages.

It's not only for students but parents too,
We want them to learn as the children must do.
They can help their children to learn with ease,
And when they come home, they'll never have Cs.

We believe students can succeed if they read,
And understand how we planted the seed.
That life is worth living and in themselves they must believe.
For this is the thought that they must conceive.

Learn to be
The Master Student

How To Develop Self-Confidence and
Effective Study Skills

By Robert Rooney and Anthony Lipuma

Illustrated by Jessica de Silva

Learn to be
The Master Student

How To Develop Self-Confidence and
Effective Study Skills

By Robert Rooney and Anthony Lipuma

Published by: **Maydale Publishing Company, Inc.**
P. O. Box 10359
Silver Spring, MD 20914

Library of Congress Catalog Card Number 92-80281

Publisher's Cataloging in Publication Data
Rooney, Robert L., 1947-
  Learn to be the master student: how to develop self-confidence and effective study skills / Robert Rooney, Anthony Lipuma
  p. cm.
  Includes bibliographical references.
  Includes index.
  ISBN 0-9632530-8-5

  1. Study, Method of. 2. Students--Life skills guides. I. Lipuma, Anthony C., 1951- II. Title. III. Title: How to develop self-confidence and effective study skills.

LB 1049.R66 1992   371.302'81
                                                    QBI92-10380

Cover design by Scott Baur Associates.

For our parents

Janice and Herb Rooney

Sue and Charles Lipuma

ACKNOWLEDGEMENTS

Special thanks are due to Pat Lipuma, Herb Rooney, Mike Hancock, Dick and Pam Cook, Jessica de Silva, Scott Baur, and others who provided valuable advice and counsel during the preparation of this book.

For the privilege of reprinting portions of selected works in this book, thanks are due to:

Blue Mountain Arts for permission to reprint poems by Laine Parsons, Michael Rille and Amanda Pierce, copyright 1983 by Blue Mountain Arts.

Nightingale-Conant, 7300 North Lehigh Avenue, Chicago, IL 60648, for permission to reprint a selection from *Lead the Field* by Earl Nightingale.

Random House, Inc. for permission to reprint a quotation from *2715 One-Line Quotations for Speakers, Writers, and Raconteurs*, by Edward P. Murphy, copyright 1981.

Simon & Schuster for permission to reprint a portion of *PSYCHO-CYBERNETICS*, by Maxwell Maltz, M.D., F.I.C.S., copyright 1960, 1968. Reprinted by permission of the publisher Prentice-Hall, Inc., a Division of Simon & Schuster, New York.

Penguin USA for permission to reprint selections from *Think and Grow Rich* by Napoleon Hill. Copyright 1937, 1960, 1966, 1967 by the Napoleon Hill Foundation. Used by permission of the publisher, Dutton, an imprint of New American Library, a division of Penguin Books USA Inc.

The Washington Post Company for permission to reprint a portion of an article on the seventh consecutive 1991 win of the Washington Redskins.

ABOUT THE AUTHORS...

Robert Rooney is a former high school counselor and is currently a successful sales representative. Mr. Rooney's unique blend of counseling experience and motivational sales training was instrumental in developing *Learn to be The Master Student.*

Anthony Lipuma is a Certified Public Accountant. Mr. Lipuma developed his own study system to successfully pass the CPA exam, perhaps the most difficult of all professional examinations. He developed an effective study system for his children and used the confidence building techniques presented in the book to improve their academic and sports performance.

TABLE OF CONTENTS

*Multiple Choice Exams * Do Not Look At The Answers * Multiple Choice Answers Are Really True/False Questions * Look For Conditional and Absolute Words * Know The Penalty for Guessing * Record Your Answers Carefully * Do Not Change Your Answers*

*Essay Exams * Answer All Questions * Plan And Outline Your Answer * Write Neatly And Legibly * Check Your Grammar, Spelling and Punctuation * Use Pencil: Write On Every Other Line*

*True/False Exams * Short Answer Exams * Matching Exams * Summary*

I bargained with Life for a penny,
And Life would pay no more,
However I begged at evening
When I counted my scanty store;

For Life is a just employer,
He gives you what you ask,
But once you have set the wages,
Why, you must bear the task.

I worked for a menial's hire,
Only to learn, dismayed,
That any wage I had asked of Life,
Life would have paid.

Jessie B. Rittenhouse

INTRODUCTION

The purpose of *Learn to be The Master Student* is to demonstrate that virtually everyone can reach high levels of achievement. The book combines techniques for developing **self-confidence** and meaningful goals with effective study skills and strategies. Your ability to excel **depends on believing** you can reach any realistic goal you desire.

A strong analogy can be drawn between reaching academic goals and athletics. In any sport, a team must have the desire to win. The coach draws up plans to enable the team to reach its goals. The team practices the plans again and again to become confident the plans can be executed effectively. So it is with academics. You must have a blueprint or plan to achieve your goals.

The authors are your coaches and this book is your blueprint for winning. After you read the book, it is up to you to follow through and get on the winning track. You must persevere. Periodically review the information presented to help you stay on track. The authors know the techniques presented in this book work: they have studied them, practiced them, and achieved their own goals using them.

The book contains three major sections: The Apprentice, The Journeyman and The Master Student. An *apprentice* is a person who is just beginning to learn a craft, trade, or line of work. A *journeyman* is someone who has completed a basic course of training but is not yet outstanding in his/her work. A *master* is someone who is practiced, skilled and recognized as outstanding in his/her work. Each section of *Learn to be The Master Student* represents a stage of development and provides information essential for *any* student to reach his or her academic, professional or personal goals.

SECTION I: THE APPRENTICE
YOUR THOUGHTS ARE THE KEY

Desire and *self-image* (beliefs about your capabilities), *directly affect* your level of achievement in any endeavor. This section discusses how your self-image affects your performance and how you can improve your self-image. Understanding and improving the self-image, coupled with effective goal setting, is the *foundation* for outstanding achievement. To attain a high level of achievement, you must believe you are capable.

SECTION II - THE JOURNEYMAN
UNDERSTANDING YOUR BODY AND MIND

To be at your peak mentally, you must be at your peak physically. This section discusses the need to understand the relationship between the body's need for rest and the ability to think and learn effectively. This section also examines how your memory functions and how to improve it. If you have experienced the nightmare of forgetting important information during an examination, you know how vital memory is to academic achievement. Your mind must provide the information you need *when* you need it.

SECTION III: THE MASTER STUDENT USING STRATEGIES AND SKILLS TO EXCEL

Effective study strategies and skills make learning easier, fun, and will almost certainly guarantee higher grades. This section discusses strategies to plan and organize your work, and the vital skills needed to reach your goals.

The subjects covered include the importance of effective reading; the need for a superior vocabulary; the need for a schedule and proper environment for studying; effective note-taking techniques; and, how to prepare for and take examinations.

To get the greatest benefit from reading the book, follow these few instructions. *First, read the table of contents* to find out what the book contains and how it is arranged. *Second, skim the entire book page by page*, reading the major titles and subtitles of each section. *Third, begin your reading* and studying of each chapter.

Before reading each chapter, (1) skim the material in the chapter, (2) read the questions at the beginning of the chapter and try to answer them as you read, and (3) read the summary at the end of the chapter. This process will increase your understanding and retention of the material presented. As you read, you will be an *active* participant. You will read later in Chapter 10 that these steps are techniques to increase the effectiveness of studying.

It is widely believed that instead of studying harder, students should study smarter. By examining and understanding your self-image, your memory, and the many study techniques available, you *will* study smarter. By using the techniques presented in this book, you *will* reach your goals and achieve far beyond what you thought was possible. You will be *The Master Student*.

Should ye see afar off that worth winning,
Set out on the journey with trust;
And ne'er heed if your path at beginning
Should be among brambles and dust.
Though it is but by footsteps ye do it.
And hardships may hinder and stay,
Walk with faith, and be sure you'll get
through it;
For "Where there's a will there's a way."

Eliza Cook

SECTION I: THE APPRENTICE

YOUR THOUGHTS ARE THE KEY

As you begin your journey, you will learn and understand how your way of thinking about yourself, your life, and your environment, affects your ability to achieve.

Whatever the mind of man can conceive and believe,
it can achieve.

Napoleon Hill

Chapter One

SELF-IMAGE: THE KEY TO ACHIEVEMENT

What is self-image? How does someone acquire their self-image, and how can it be changed? How long does it take to change a self-image? How can someone maintain a strong self-image?

Understanding The Self-Image

Your self-image is your complete picture of yourself. It is developed over your lifetime and it includes your ***beliefs about your capabilities***, as well as your attitudes and feelings. If necessary, you can change your self-image through realization, desire, goal setting, and faith. You must (1) ***realize*** that you can change, (2) ***desire*** to change, (3) ***set goals***, and (4) ***have faith*** in your ability to reach your goals. It takes at least *twenty-one days* to affect any change in behavior or habit. Therefore, you can expect it may take about twenty-one days to change your self-image once you begin to practice the necessary techniques. You might not notice the change, but it will be apparent to others. Sometimes it takes the comments of others to make you realize the difference.

To maintain a strong self-image, you must adopt a positive attitude. Next, dwell on your accomplishments instead of your failures. Finally, ***reject*** the insults to your self-image heaped upon you by others. Consider two people, Bill and Mary, and their respective self-images.

Mary is a high school senior. She sees herself as intelligent and highly motivated. Mary knows that she can excel in any class, and her grades reinforce this picture of herself. Most of her friends are good students, and they often work together on school assignments. Her ambition is to attend college and become a doctor, specifically a pediatrician. Mary also sees herself as a happy, outgoing, loving, and considerate person.

Bill has never thought of himself as intelligent. He has had trouble understanding math since elementary school. Once, when he could not answer a simple math problem, another student called him stupid. He is now in the eleventh grade, and Bill genuinely believes he *is* stupid when it comes to math. He usually gets a *D*. His grades in other subjects are a little better than math, but not much better. He manages to get an occasional *B*, but mostly *Cs* in the rest of his subjects.

Bill's grades reinforce his picture of himself as lacking intelligence. Most of his friends receive the same grades. Bill and his friends like school for the social environment it provides; however, they consider much of what they learn to be useless for later in life. Bill does not know what he wants to do or what he wants to be after he graduates from high school. He has not seriously thought about going to college, and does not believe he could get accepted because of his low grades. Most of his friends are not going to college, so he believes he is in good company.

As you can see, these people have two very different self-images of themselves. Mary is confident, has established goals and is motivated to achieve her goals. She appears destined for success.

Although you may not have established a goal as specific as Mary's, do not be discouraged. It may take time and research to decide upon a suitable goal.

Bill, on the other hand, has little self-confidence, no goals, and, as a result, is not motivated to achieve anything specific. Bill is actually afraid to set goals for himself because he does not believe he can achieve them. He appears destined for mediocrity. Can Bill possibly turn his life around and become a self-confident, motivated student destined for greatness?

 The answer is a resounding *yes*! Bill can improve, he can succeed! Bill's current self-image consists of ***erroneous beliefs*** about what he is and what he can do. He has formed these beliefs over his lifetime. His poor grades and negative comments from his parents and teachers have reinforced these beliefs. Within Bill, however, lies the ***potential*** to achieve. His challenge is to ***bridge the gap*** between what he ***believes*** he is, as opposed to what he ***can be***. Unfortunately, Bill has not yet discovered the secret to tap this potential.

What is this secret and how can Bill use it to his advantage? Not surprisingly, the secret is contained within Bill's mind, and it is the ***power of his own thoughts***. Bill's thoughts, which are translated into his self-image, continually reinforce his belief that he is a *C* student, that "he is not good at math," and that "he is not an intelligent person." These dominant thoughts naturally cause him to affirm his image of himself through his poor performance in school. He spends little time studying: he believes that even if he did study more, his grades would not improve. Bill's thoughts about himself limit his ability to achieve. These thoughts are called self-limiting beliefs.

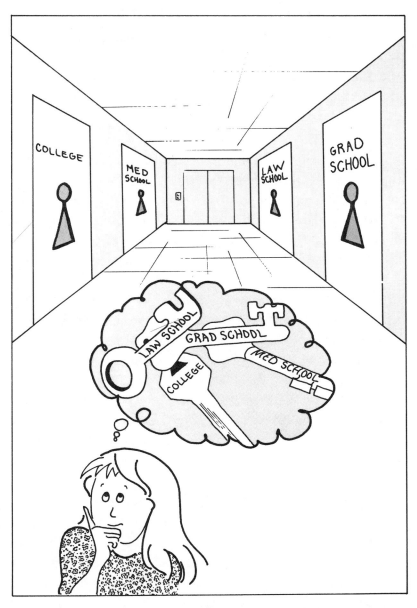

YOUR THOUGHTS ARE THE KEY TO SUCCESS

Conquering Self-limiting Beliefs

Exactly what are "self-limiting beliefs?" How do people acquire such beliefs? How can you eliminate "self-limiting" beliefs?

Have you ever noticed a circus elephant tethered with a rope? Tethered with a rope! How ridiculous! Why, that elephant could snap the rope and go anywhere it wishes. Right? Wrong! It is true that the elephant is powerful and has the *ability* to break the rope, but it cannot. Why? Examine the situation a bit more closely.

When the elephant was a baby, it was tethered with a heavy chain to a spike sunk in concrete. No matter how hard it tried, the baby elephant could not break away. Eventually, the elephant gave up trying to break away because it knew it could not. Later, instead of using the heavy chain and a spike sunk in concrete, the owners used a rope attached to a stake driven into the ground. Although it has the *ability* to get away, it does not try because it *believes* it cannot. The elephant has a self-limiting belief that it cannot break the rope and get away.

In *PSYCHO-CYBERNETICS*, Dr. Maxwell Maltz discusses his own examples of self-limiting beliefs. He describes situations where, under hypnosis, people are told they cannot do things they normally can do. A hypnotist tells a football player he cannot lift his hand from a table. As hard as he tries, the football player cannot seem to lift his hand. The hypnotist tells a championship weight-lifter that he cannot lift a pencil from a desk. Although he can usually lift several hundred pounds, the weight-lifter cannot lift the pencil.

Under hypnosis these athletes have the same physical *ability*. There is an important difference, however. Under hypnosis, they *believe* they cannot perform. This *belief* overrides their physical *ability* to react. Thus, your *beliefs* about your *abilities* can prevent you from attaining outstanding achievement. It is unfortunate that these erroneous beliefs can keep you from greatness.

Developing Desire: The Starting Point for Achievement

The widely held belief of eminent psychologists and authors is that people become what they think about. When you *desire* something strongly enough and think about it often, you are likely to attain it. You have already seen how your thoughts can limit your ability to achieve. When you believe you cannot do something, you generally will not be able to do it. In academics, if you think of yourself as a *C* or *D* student, then that *is* what you *will be*. See yourself as an *A* or *B* student, and that is what you will be.

In *The One Minute Teacher*, Spencer and Constance Johnson point out that the primary cause of not learning is having a poor self-image, not a lack of ability. Negative and destructive thoughts result in a poor self-image.

In *PSYCHO-CYBERNETICS*, Dr. Maltz explains that

> The "self-image" sets the boundaries of individual accomplishment. It defines what you can and cannot do. Expand the self image and you expand the "area of the possible." The development of an adequate, realistic self-image will seem to imbue the individual with new capabilities, new talents and literally turn failure into success.

So how do you "literally turn failure into success?" The first step to changing your dominant self-image is a strong desire to change. It is not enough for someone such as Bill to say, "I think I want to be an *A* student." You must use all the mental power you can muster. You must decide *to be* an *A* student. You must have a burning desire to reach this goal. You must *see* yourself as already being an *A* student. You must use your *imagination* and vividly picture yourself achieving this goal, thereby convincing your subconscious that you have achieved.

Using Imagination and
Visualization

Your self-image is stored in your subconscious mind. The subconscious works twenty-four hours a day.   It is working while you are at school or work, and all night while you are sleeping. During sleep, it is sorting and evaluating the information that has come through your conscious mind during the day.   It is also responsible for your dreams.

The subconscious mind is your automatic pilot. It keeps you on course based upon what it believes to be true and real. You may exert some extra effort and get better grades for a short time.   Eventually, however, your subconscious mind will bring you back to where it "believes" you should be, for example getting *Cs* and *Ds*.

Imagine the conflict within someone who is trying to quit smoking. The conscious mind wants to quit because it knows that smoking is unhealthy.   The subconscious, however, sees the person as a smoker. The self-image must be changed. This is why it is difficult to reach any goal by sheer willpower alone. The goal of your conscious mind conflicts with the image contained in the subconscious.

So how do you break this cycle? Simply by conditioning your subconscious so that it begins to see a new self-image, a new picture of self.   For example, see yourself as someone who consistently gets *As* and *Bs*. See yourself as a non-smoker.

Now, how do you condition the subconscious to develop this new picture? You do it through *imagination and visualization*.

An amazing fact about the subconscious mind is that it cannot tell the difference between a real event and a vividly imagined event. While this sounds eerie, it is true. If you doubt this, try the following experiment. Have someone read the following paragraph (slowly) as you close your eyes and sit relaxed.

Imagine that it is a hot summer day. You've just arrived home and are about to enter the house. See yourself at your front door. Put your key in the lock. Turn the doorknob and open the door. As you step inside, you feel the cool rush of air on your face. You're glad you put the air conditioning on last night. Your feet are burning up, so you take off your shoes and socks and leave them by the door. The cool floor soothes your burning feet. You walk into the kitchen and open the refrigerator. You feel the cool air as you open the door. You reach down and open the fruit bin and see a big, yellow lemon. You take the lemon and close the door. You put the lemon on a cutting board and cut it into quarters. OOPS! A squirt hits you in the eye! Take a piece of lemon and smell it. Now, take a big bite of the lemon, sinking your teeth deep into it.

Well, what was your reaction? Did your lips pucker, did your saliva start flowing? Of course it did! And you only took an imaginary bite of lemon. Imagination triggered an actual physical response. Convinced about the power of your thoughts? Not yet? Okay, read the next example taken from an actual psychological study.

A psychologist conducted an experiment to determine if mental practice could improve performance. The experiment involved three groups of students throwing basketball free throws. Each group was tested at the beginning and end of a twenty day period. The first group practiced twenty minutes a day. The second group did not practice at all. The third group spent twenty minutes a day *imagining and visualizing* they were shooting successful free throws. The results seem amazing. The first group, which practiced, improved its performance twenty-four per

cent. The second group, which did not practice, showed no improvement. The third group, which practiced in their imagination, improved twenty-three per cent! The process of vivid imagination translated thoughts into action.

So what is the purpose of learning about lemons and basketballs? Once you understand that your thoughts can be converted into actions, there is no limit to what you can accomplish. You can be anything you want to be if you first mentally see yourself reach your goal. It is vital that the imagined experience be vivid and emotional. As you imagine yourself reaching a goal, you must *feel and experience* the *excitement* of reaching the goal, as though you have already done it. This is the technique used by top athletes prior to a competition. They visualize a successful performance *before* the actual competition.

Developing Faith And
Self-Confidence

Imagining and visualizing achievement also allows you to develop faith and confidence in your ability to reach a goal. Every time you *see* yourself reaching the goal, it reinforces the thought that you have achieved.

You also develop faith and self-confidence by consciously choosing to recall the successes of your life and by mentally refusing to dwell on failures. When failures occur, analyze your mistakes to avoid them in the future. You *learn* by making mistakes. It is a natural part of life. Therefore, it serves no useful purpose to dwell continually on mistakes and failures and berate yourself because of them. They are in the past, and you cannot change what has happened. If you dwell on failure, this is precisely what you can expect to receive in the future.

Anthony Robbins, a well known lecturer and author on the subject of self-development and improvement, hammers home the point *"The past does not equal the future."* In other words, the future is not tied to the past. It can be what you want it to be.

 Failures are merely detours on the road to reaching your goals. As with a detour, it may take a little longer to get there, but eventually you will. You need to view failures as temporary setbacks and nothing more. Thomas Edison failed many times before he discovered a proper filament for the incandescent light bulb. Have you ever

SEE YOURSELF ATTAIN YOUR GOALS

watched olympic figure skaters? When they perform their routines, they complete their program even if they take a fall. *They do not quit!* They get up and continue to put forth their best effort until their program is finished. Students can learn a valuable lesson from observing the dedication and persistence of these athletes.

Listed below are some examples of famous people who refused to allow failure to gain a foothold on their lives. Consider the following example and ask yourself if you would give up if the same misfortunes fell upon you.

> This person's mother died when he was a small boy. As he grew older, he and his sister became very close. However, she died in childbirth at a young age. He ran for a seat in the state legislature but he was defeated. He became a businessman and failed. His fiancee died. He ran for Congress and was defeated. He ran for Congress again, and this time was elected; however, he was again defeated two years later. He was an unsuccessful candidate for the Vice-Presidency. Despite the tragedies and bitter disappointments in his life, he became perhaps the most outstanding president of the United States. The man was Abraham Lincoln.

In his *Personal Power* tape program, Anthony Robbins tells a humorous story relating how Colonel Sanders, of Kentucky Fried Chicken fame, got started. It seems that Colonel Sanders reached the age of sixty-five and decided that he could not live on Social Security. So, he came up with the idea of selling his chicken recipe to people in exchange for a commission on all the chicken these people would ever sell. The Colonel had a hard time because many people he approached thought he was crazy. However, the Colonel pressed on. In fact, Colonel Sanders was rejected over 1,000 times before he finally succeeded in selling the recipe. Few people would have the courage and determination to press on after so many rejections.

Helen Keller became deaf, dumb, and blind shortly after birth and accomplished more in her lifetime than most people without handicaps. She is, without doubt, one of the most inspirational persons to have ever lived.

Two more dramatic examples are also worth mentioning. Which names come to mind when you think of the greatest baseball players of all time? Babe Ruth certainly has to be one. Did you know that Babe Ruth struck out more times than he hit home runs? Although his lifetime batting average was over .300, he failed about seventy per cent of the times he came up to bat! Carl Yastremski, the Boston Red Sox great, also hit better than .300 during his lifetime. The fact that he, too, failed seventy per cent of the times he came to bat did not diminish his opinion of his ability. Both "Babe" and "Yaz" had high expectations of themselves; they knew they could achieve, and they did!

As a student, the situation is the same, although you cannot afford to fail seventy per cent of the time. You must not allow present or past failures to affect your future efforts. You develop faith and self confidence by accumulating a series of successful acts and by dwelling on the positive results. You must have *faith* in your *ability*. You must *expect* to reach your goal.

To conclude this discussion, consider a finding made by the U. S. Department of Education in its 1987 study, *What Works- -Research About Teaching and Learning.* "Students who *believe* they can succeed are usually more successful than those with low self-esteem when it comes to participating in activities, working independently, getting along with others, and *achieving academically."*

Rejecting Challenges
To Your Self-Esteem

As you establish a new self-image, you begin to develop a keen sense of self-esteem. This sense of self-esteem comes from your belief in yourself and your faith that you can accomplish your goals. With self-esteem comes an attitude of confidence and an ability to interact effectively with others. People with high self-esteem have positive attitudes and expect good things from life. The person with high self-esteem is confident, yet modest. You cannot treat others with dignity and respect if you do not have dignity and respect for yourself. But even with high self-esteem, you must be careful not to get *sniooped*. SNIOOPED?

In his motivational classic, *Think and Grow Rich*, Napoleon Hill admonishes his readers not to be Susceptible to the

Negative Influences Of Other People (SNIOOPed). His message is that you must not allow other people to affect your faith and confidence in yourself. You *must reject* challenges to your self-esteem.

Where do these challenges to your self-esteem come from? They can come from anywhere, from your family, friends, teachers, co-workers and others. For example, you might see yourself as a student with a 3.5 grade point average. As you work toward this average, you might tell someone about your goal. Upon hearing this, they promptly reply, "You'll never do that, you're not smart enough." Or perhaps, "You've never received above 2.5 before, what makes you think you can do it now?"

Your rejection does not have to be overt or confrontational. You can reject such challenges in your mind. Since *you* have exclusive control of your thoughts, you have the *power* to do this. Napoleon Hill profoundly asserted that "no one is ever defeated until defeat is accepted as reality."

Stand and Deliver

To fully appreciate the relationship of desire and determination to academic achievement, consider the experience of Jaime Escalante, a Los Angeles mathematics teacher. Escalante's story is told in a Warner Home Video entitled *Stand and Deliver*. It is one of the most inspirational stories you can ever experience!

Escalante was assigned to teach basic math at Garfield High School. His students came from an impoverished area of the city and few, if any, had a desire to learn math or any other subject. When he began, his students' math skills were far below the high school level. He started teaching them fractions. Later, he convinced them they were too smart for simple math and began teaching them algebra. Eventually, when Escalante had instilled desire, courage and perseverance in his students, he taught them calculus. With their desire and new-found belief in themselves, his students took and passed the Advanced Placement Calculus Examination. The fact that all who took the exam passed was an unheard of achievement, particularly from a school on its way to academic oblivion!

Escalante's experience is *proof* that past performance is not indicative of future achievement, and that believing in yourself can work what may appear to be miracles and bring academic riches!

Summary

Your *self-image* is the collection of beliefs about yourself that you have acquired over your lifetime. Your self-image defines the boundaries of potential accomplishment. With a good self-image and a positive outlook, you can achieve almost anything you desire; with a poor self-image and a negative outlook, any accomplishment will be difficult.

You must understand that you have the potential to achieve beyond what you believe is possible. Your challenge is to *bridge the gap* between what you *think you are*, as opposed to *what you can be*. You must not allow erroneous or *self-limiting* beliefs to stifle your ability to achieve. Just because your grade point average (GPA) has never been above 2.5 *does not* mean that you *are* a 2.5 GPA student. You can achieve a 3.0, 3.5 or higher GPA. What you have done in the past *is not* indicative of your potential for the future.

To achieve beyond your present status, you must have the *desire* to go further. You cannot simply hope or wish to achieve more. You must use your *imagination* to *visualize* yourself being where you want to be. When you see yourself as winner, as someone who has reached his or her goal, the actual task of achieving becomes easier.

You must maintain your *faith and self-confidence* in yourself. Focus on and think about your strengths. Recall your past successes and refuse to dwell on your failures. Failures have their own purposes; they teach what does not work. Failures are detours. You will reach your destination but it will take a bit longer.

Finally, *reject challenges to your self-esteem*. Do not allow others to tamper with the faith and confidence you have in yourself. There may be times when others mean to criticize your behavior, but instead they criticize you as a person. *No one* has the right to demean your person.

*It's natural to feel disappointed
when things don't go your way
It's easy to think...
"I can't do it, so why try?"
But, no matter how scared you are
of making a mistake
or how discouraged you may become,
Never give up...
because if you don't try and
if you don't go after what you want in life,
it won't come to you,
and you'll be forced to accept
things that you know could
be better...
Success is not measured by
whether you win or
whether you fail-
there's always a little bit
of success, even if things
don't go your way -
What's important is that you'll
feel better about yourself,
for the simple reason
that you tried.*

Amanda Pierce

Chapter Two

SUCCESS: A NEW DEFINITION

What is true *success*? How is *success* defined? How does one go about achieving *success*?

Create A New State Of Mind

Success is defined as *"the accomplishment of what is desired or aimed at, achievement, military success, academic success; attainment of wealth, fame, prosperity, etc."*[1] You normally believe you achieve success when you *reach* a goal. You associate success with the end product of your labors. This way of thinking implies you are not yet successful, so you are constantly chasing success. Getting good grades does bring a measure of success. However, to reach your goal, you must *be successful* every step of the way. This is the true nature of success.

In *Lead The Field*, noted lecturer Earl Nightingale says that the best definition of success he ever heard was that *"Success is the progressive realization of a worthy goal."* This definition implies that while you *continually* pursue any goal, you are by definition successful. Your goals will become easier to achieve, because you know that living successfully, doing everything you can each day, brings you one step closer to the goal. So commit now to think of success in terms of everyday living, and not in terms of ultimately reaching your goal. In a previous section on imagination and visualization, you learned about the importance of seeing yourself as having already attained your goal. This process of imagining and visualizing requires much less effort when you are already working as *best* as you can to reach the goal.

Nightingale compares this idea of successful living to building a house. When you begin, you literally have thousands of bricks to put into place. When you work carefully and methodically, you put one brick after another in place doing as much as you can, as *best* as you can, day after day until the job is completed. You will reach your goal and complete the house because you acted successfully each step of the way. This analogy holds true for academics as it does for anything you do in life. Noted Harvard psychologist and author, William James, observed that if students will do the best they can each day, they will reach their goals.

Summary

The dictionary definition of success states that it is the end product of attempts to reach a goal. This implies that while striving to attain a goal you are not yet successful. Nothing could be further from the truth.

While you are actively engaged in pursuing any worthwhile goal, you *are* *successful*. This necessarily implies acting successfully every step of the way. To be a successful student, you must have a good self-image and a positive attitude; you must have  clear goals; you must learn and practice the proper strategies and skills; you must complete your assignments on-time; and, you must adequately prepare for your classes and examinations. These attitudes and actions require your attention every day.

When you adopt this new view of success you do not have to wait for good grades to be a success. *You are a success* because you have *exerted your best effort* each step of the way!

PERFORM EACH TASK, ONE AT A TIME

To reach my goals, what I want to be,
I first must start with learning to see,
The ability I have, not what others perceive;
Because it's only myself that I can deceive.

When I've accepted myself, my faults in all,
I'll know I can't take a permanent fall.
I can set a course and then begin,
A brand new life, one that's destined to win.

I'll take each job, each task, each chore,
And perform each step until there are no more.
This is the way I'll reach my goals,
And keep good company with determined souls.

Anthony Lipuma

Chapter Three

GOALS: SETTING A NEW DIRECTION

What are goals? Why is it important to have goals? How does one choose goals? What is the process for setting and achieving goals?

Establish Specific Goals

A goal can be something you want to become or something you want to do. You might want to become a teacher or take a trip around the world. Setting and reaching goals (spiritual, emotional, academic, professional, etc.) is what makes you a happy and effective human being.

When you set goals, you set a definite course for your life and give it direction. Without goals, your life is like a ship without a rudder. You drift from place to place without real accomplishment in any area. Imagine how ridiculous a football game would be if a team could not find the goal. Consider a discussion that took place between one of the authors, Tony, and his friend. They concluded that when goals are clear, definite and specific, they are easier to attain.

Tony and his friend were discussing the quality of the undergraduate education they received from the same public university. They were average students and did not believe the quality of their education was good. They wondered if a private college or university would have assured a better education. As undergraduates, they had no specific employment goals after graduation.

Several years later, they went back to school. Tony's friend enrolled in a private college to obtain a Masters degree in special education. Tony attended the same public university to obtain accounting credits. Their academic results on returning to school were dramatically different. They achieved all *As* and *Bs* and believed the quality of the education they received was much better the second time around. How did this happen since his friend attended a private school, and Tony attended the same public university?

The answer is simple. Upon returning to school they had clearly defined goals. They knew *why* they were in school and what they hoped to achieve. For Tony's friend, the Masters degree meant increased status and an almost immediate increase in salary. What an incentive! Tony needed accounting credits to qualify for the Certified Public Accountant (CPA) exam. Passing the CPA exam meant an immediate increase in marketable skills and becoming a member of a recognized profession.

Because they had clearly defined goals on their "second tour" of college, they were genuinely interested in their education. They had an incentive. *They wanted to learn!*

They concluded that it did not matter what school they attended. To be sure, some schools and teachers are better than others. However, it was the desire to reach their respective goals, their motivation, that made the difference.

Think of your own life. Think of the large or small projects that you completed. It could have been a school project or hobby. Relive the enjoyment you experienced while working on the project. Didn't the project give you a sense of direction, a sense of purpose? Relive the satisfaction you felt when you completed the project. Don't you feel that sense of accomplishment, that sense of pride and self-worth for a job well done? This is what effective goal setting can do for you.

Understanding The Types Of Goals

You should set short-term, mid-term and long-term goals. You must plan for the immediate, intermediate and distant future. For example, a short-term goal might be to raise your grade point average by the next grading period. An intermediate goal might be to become an honor student. A long term goal might be to become a member of a profession, a doctor or teacher, for example.

Setting Effective Goals

All goals have certain characteristics to make their achievement possible.

Goals must be clearly stated. You must understand why the goal is important to you. For example, it is not sufficient to say "My goal is to get good grades." Getting good grades is a noble goal, but why is getting good grades important? Do you want the grades to get into a specific high school or college? Do you want the grades because you feel a sense of personal pride and achievement when you get these grades? Knowing why the goal is important to you is vital to maintaining a level of excitement and enthusiasm while working toward the goal.

Goals must be specific and measurable. You might set your goal to become a *B* student. However, a *B* student's grade point average could be from 3.0 to 3.99. Select a specific average as your target. In this way, you can measure your progress as your grade point average rises during the school year. When you set a specific average as a goal, you will know exactly when you arrive.

Goals must be challenging. It might seem as though the goal is just out of reach, but you can achieve it if you try hard enough. It serves no useful purpose to set a goal you know you can achieve with little effort. Suppose you have a high *C* or about a 2.8 grade point average. You know that with just a little more effort you can get a 3.0 or *B* average. While getting your grades up to a *B* average is indeed an accomplishment, how much self-satisfaction can this bring? Why not go for a 3.5 average? This average might enable you to get into a prestigious school, if that is your goal. Such an average might open the opportunity to attend honors classes and further expand your knowledge and potential. Set goals that seem just out of reach. As you achieve these goals, you can set new goals and go on to higher levels of achievement.

Goals must have time limits. When do you want to reach your goal? Can you wait five years? Must you reach it by the end of the grading period? Definite time limits provide you with the added motivation to get the job done, to achieve, to reach your goal.

Goals must be reviewed periodically. You must decide if they are still appropriate for your situation. For example, as you attain your goals you should set new ones. When was the last time you reviewed your goals?

Goals must be written. When you write down your goals you free your mind to concentrate on how to reach them. When goals are written, they become concrete instead of abstract. You can *see* them.

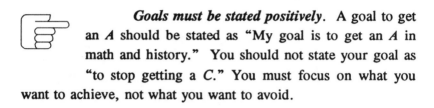 *Goals must be stated positively.* A goal to get an *A* should be stated as "My goal is to get an *A* in math and history." You should not state your goal as "to stop getting a *C*." You must focus on what you want to achieve, not what you want to avoid.

Reinforce And Affirm Your Goals: The Goal Card

Did you know that noted success researchers estimate that only five per cent of the population is working toward clear, definite goals? The rest are drifting along aimlessly. They only take advantage of whatever "happens" to come their way. People spend more time planning goals for their vacations than they do planning goals for their lives.

By contrast, the top five per cent have determined what they want from life. They are actively pursuing their goals.

When you set clear, definite goals you immediately place yourself in the top five per cent.

You should affirm your goals several times a day, preferably out loud. You do this by having your goals written on a card that you carry with you at all times. The goals will become a part of you. Stating your goals aloud is important. When doing so, you take advantage of two senses, sight and hearing, to reinforce your determination to reach them. When you use more than one sense, you imbed the thought and determination more deeply into your subconscious mind.

The best time to affirm your goals is when you are relaxed. Your subconscious mind is more receptive to suggestion at this time. A good time of day to affirm goals is just after arising and just before falling asleep.

You can also affirm your goals at other times during the day. With your goal card in hand, you can review it (silently) while you are waiting for the bus, when you are on the bus, and anytime when you have a few moments between activities. You can do it privately, without disturbing anyone, or drawing attention to yourself.

When you are at home, in your room or even your car, you can state your goals aloud. In the car, of course, you can state your goals without actually reading them. You will no doubt have them memorized. Who cares if someone in the next car sees you? You might feel a bit uncomfortable, however, if you are verbalizing your goals at a traffic light and have the windows down.

Reward Yourself For Reaching Your Goals

Human beings are no different from other creatures. We like to be rewarded for a job well done. Have you ever observed an animal trainer after the animal has performed successfully? The trainer rewards the animal with a treat. This action reinforces the animal's positive behavior.

You, too, should be rewarded. You might tell yourself that on reaching a goal, you will buy a new tape, some new clothes, or anything else you might want. How you reward yourself is not important. It is important to know that you can look forward to a reward, and when you receive it, you will know that you deserved it.

Setting and Reaching Daily Goals: Defeating Procrastination

Besides setting short-term, intermediate, and long-term goals, you also must plan to accomplish your daily goals or tasks. A tremendously effective way to achieve daily goals is to use a 3x5 card to list the six most important tasks to complete tomorrow. List each task in its order of importance. Do this each night before you go to bed.

You can divide your tasks into categories and list the six most important personal, academic, or work related goals. Tomorrow, begin working on the first task until you successfully complete it. Next, go on to number two and so on. If you do not complete all six (or however many from each category), carry the remaining tasks (goals) forward to the next day. Cross out or check off each goal as you complete it. This method of achieving daily goals brings satisfaction and order to your life. You will defeat any tendency to procrastinate.

Often, you can be overwhelmed by all the tasks you have to accomplish. If you follow the approach explained, you *will* complete each task in its order of priority. As you check or cross each one off your list, you will *see* your accomplishments. You will feel successful. You will feel the satisfaction that comes from completing each task to the best your ability.

Imagine going to the grocery store without a list. You will waste time just trying to recall the items. Ultimately, the trip will take longer and you will be distracted and buy things you do not need. If you use a list, however, you could finish the task *quickly, without distraction*, and proceed to the *next task*.

Summary

Goals provide a *direction and purpose* for your life. It is difficult to stay motivated and maintain an interest in school if you do not see a reason for being there. When you have a reason, when you develop goals, your studies become interesting because you *want to learn*.

To be effective, goals must (1) *be stated clearly*, (2) *be challenging*, (3) *have time limits for accomplishment*, (4) *be reviewed periodically*, (5) *be written*, and (6) *be stated positively*. You should set short-term, mid-term, and long-term goals.

To affirm and state your goals frequently, write them on a card that you can review several times a day. When you reach a goal, reward yourself.

You should set daily goals to accomplish the things you must do each day. Before bedtime, write down the most important things you must do tomorrow, in the order of their importance. As you accomplish each task, cross it off your list. This process will help you to see your achievements and defeat a fierce enemy: *procrastination*.

It ain't the failures he may meet,
That keeps a man from winnin',
It's the discouragement complete
That blocks a new beginnin';
You want to quit your habit bad,
And, when the shadows flittin'
Make life seem worthless an' sad,
You want to quit your quittin'!

You may want to quit-a-layin' down
An sayin' hope is over,
Because the fields are bare an' brown
Where once we lived in clover.
When jolted from the water cart
It's painful to be hittin'
The earth; but make another start.
Cheer up, and quit your quittin'!

Although the games seems rather stiff
Don't be a doleful doubter;
There's always one more innin' if
You're not a down-and-outer.
But fortune's pretty sure to flee
From folks content with sittin'
Around an sayin' life's N. G.
You've got to quit your quittin'.

Unknown

Chapter Four

MOTIVATION: MOTIVATING YOURSELF

What is motivation? Can others motivate you? How can you motivate yourself?

Understanding Motivation

At last we come to a topic that is foremost in the minds of many people, and yet it is a topic that is easily misunderstood. By having studied the previous pages, you should now realize that only *you can motivate yourself.*

When you have a positive self-image, when you have set meaningful goals, when you have a strong desire to reach your goals, and when you actively work toward your goals, you are already motivated. As you achieve your goals and as you set new goals, you become motivated to reach new heights of achievement.

Before you understood the effect of your self-image on your life, you may have believed that others could motivate you. Others can only influence you to motivate yourself. It is up to you to actually do the job. For example, your parents, friends or co-workers could suggest worthy goals or reasons to achieve; however, no motivating force takes place until you accept such suggestions as your own and begin to work earnestly toward achieving them. Read the following story and see how it applies to the concept of motivation.

> *One day a friend was admiring my garden. In particular he was admiring my corn. He said "I'd like to be able to have corn like that in my own garden." So I gave him some seed. He took the seed, then went home and threw it into his back yard. To his dismay, only a few seeds sprouted, and what did sprout did not produce very good*

corn. He asked me about this. I told him that he needed to prepare the ground, carefully place the seeds, then fertilize, and tend the plants once they start to grow. He went back to his home and carefully plowed and tilled the garden. He made even rows and fertilized the new corn as he planted it. Soon, the plants began to sprout and they were indeed healthy plants. As they grew, he pulled the weeds and watered the corn regularly, until finally he had fine a crop of corn.

Now, did my friend **make** the corn grow? Or did he provide the proper environment where the seed could prosper and grow? No one can motivate you, just as you cannot truly motivate anyone else. Others can only provide the environment, which includes encouragement and incentives for you to achieve.

Summary

Motivation results from your fervent desire to reach a stated goal. Your positive expectations about reaching the goal keep you interested and on track. No one can motivate you. Only you can motivate yourself. Family, friends, and teachers may guide and influence you to be motivated in some direction. However, it is up to you to develop the desire and to pursue a goal actively.

*A particular train of thought persisted in, be it good or bad,
cannot fail to produce its results on the character and
circumstances. People cannot directly choose their
circumstances, but they can choose their thoughts, and so
indirectly, yet surely, shape their circumstances.*

James Allen

Chapter Five

ENVIRONMENT:

THE INFLUENCE OF OTHERS

What is an environment? How does environment affect you? How can you deal with your environment?

Establish and Maintain A Positive Environment

Your environment can directly influence your level of achievement. There are many types of environments in your life. These include your family, friends, school, church, work, and others. When these environments provide a supportive and encouraging atmosphere for your development, your task of reaching your goals becomes easier. You thrive on support and encouragement, and this atmosphere stimulates you to achieve further. However, when such support and encouragement is missing, you must work harder and depend more on self-encouragement to reach your goals.

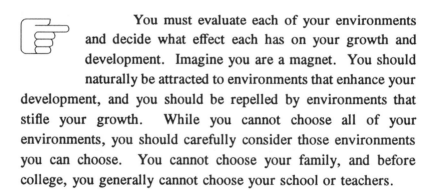
You must evaluate each of your environments and decide what effect each has on your growth and development. Imagine you are a magnet. You should naturally be attracted to environments that enhance your development, and you should be repelled by environments that stifle your growth. While you cannot choose all of your environments, you should carefully consider those environments you can choose. You cannot choose your family, and before college, you generally cannot choose your school or teachers.

There is one environment, perhaps the most important, that you can choose. That is your friends. The people with whom you associate the most. You should associate with people having goals common with your own. Imagine trying to establish a positive self-image and worthy goals, when your friends have negative attitudes and lack goals. As you work or study harder, you will be ridiculed by these "friends." You will be fighting an uphill battle trying to become what *you* desire, against what your "friends" want you to be. Just as you must refuse to dwell on past failures, you must stop associating with people who exert a negative influence on you.

Someone once said, "Association breeds assimilation." How true! The more you associate with the people around you, the more you become like them. Achieving your goals is far easier when those around you have similar goals.

Summary

Your environment consists of your family, friends, schoolmates, co-workers, neighbors and others. A positive influence from these environments will make it easier to reach your goals. You will be in contact with people who provide you with encouragement and support.

A negative influence from such environments will make reaching your goals difficult. Instead of providing encouragement, these people may actually discourage you.

While you cannot choose every environment (family, for example) you can choose your friends, those who may provide the greatest influence on your life. Choose your friends carefully and associate with those who have positive goals similar to your own.

*Set yourself earnestly
to see what you are made to do,
and then set yourself earnestly
to do it . . .
and the loftier your purpose is
the more sure you will be
to make the world richer
with every enrichment
of yourself.*

Phillips Brooks

SECTION II: THE JOURNEYMAN

UNDERSTANDING YOUR BODY
AND MIND

You have established a foundation for achievement through an understanding of your self-image and the need for goals. Now, you must understand the relationship between the body's need for rest and optimum mental performance and, how to use your memory effectively.

There is a funny old saying, one that says,
"If you don't ride a bicycle,
you don't fall off!"
What it means to say, of course, is
if you do put a lot of energy into something,
you are bound to make mistakes;
and if you take a lot of risks,
you are bound to tumble here and there.
But remember this; that if you persist
you will arrive at the destination of your choice.
And if you do occasionally fall in the process,
you'll learn much more than if you don't.

So try, and do, and discover all that you can be . . .

Michael Rille

Chapter Six

THE BODY:

YOUR RESERVOIR OF STRENGTH

What is the relationship between the body and the mind? How does a rested body affect your mental state? How does sleep affect performance?

Your Body Clock:
The Need for Sleep

Within each person is a "clock." This biological or body clock regulates your awake and sleep cycles and how you feel at different times of the day, month or year. Your daily routines help to set this body clock.

When you suddenly change your routine, your body clock fails to function properly. As a result, you will feel tired and sluggish. The most obvious example where a change in routine can upset the body clock is jet lag. When people pass through several time zones, it often takes their bodies several days to adjust to the new routine. For example, if you fly from New York to Los Angeles and arrive at 2 p.m. California time, you might feel you are ready for dinner even though it is only lunch time (by your body clock). At 8 p.m. (11 p.m. New York time), you might feel that you are ready for bed although the evening is just beginning. So, you go to bed, get eight hours of sleep and awake at three in the morning. When you wake up, it is likely you will be ready for breakfast. It will take a day or more to reset your body clock to a normal West coast schedule.

During the adjustment period, you may feel groggy and your performance is likely to be below par. This is how your body's cycles (waking, sleeping, eating) are thrown out of sync when crossing several time zones.

PAY ATTENTION TO YOUR BODY CLOCK

Although you may not have given it much thought, the same thing happens when you establish a routine during the week and stay up excessively late on the weekends. As with jet lag, your performance during the adjustment period (Saturday, Sunday, Monday and maybe even longer) will not be at its best. Therefore, it is vital that you understand the relationship between your body clock and the need to study, take examinations, or undertake other important efforts.

Whenever you anticipate a situation when you must perform at your best, you should make every effort to ensure your body clock stays on track. Thus, if you have to prepare for an examination or important meeting on Monday, you should keep your weekend activities as close to your normal schedule as possible.

It will be difficult to spend quality time studying or preparing on Saturday and Sunday if you are not fully rested. In an unrested or groggy state, preparation for your Monday activities will not be effective. Furthermore, you may not be fully rested by Monday when you must be at your best to achieve peak performance.

If you have experienced this situation, recall how you felt. You had an exam on Monday and intended to spend several hours studying on Saturday and Sunday. However, on Friday and Saturday night, you stayed up until the early morning hours partying with friends. When Saturday rolled around, and then Sunday, you had neither the inclination nor the willpower to study.

You slept late and wasted a good portion of the day when you could have spent at least some time studying.

When you finally opened the books, you quickly began to drift off into the land of nod. Because you were so tired, you could not prepare adequately. On Monday, you still felt groggy and, as a result, you were neither mentally sharp nor alert. Your grade probably reflected your level of preparation, but what could you expect: you were neither mentally nor physically prepared.

In their book, *The Secrets Our Body Clocks Reveal*, Susan Perry and Jim Dawson discuss the function and importance of sleep. In particular, they note the importance of two distinct stages of sleep, deep sleep and REM (dream) sleep. They note that deep sleep acts as a nightly tune-up restoring the body and brain. They also note the opinion of sleep researchers that REM sleep helps to consolidate memory by filing a day's experiences into the appropriate places in the brain.

REM sleep also helps to sort a day's experiences into those that must be remembered and those that can be forgotten. Dawson and Perry explain that when you disrupt your sleep cycle, you reduce the time your body spends in this stage of sleep.

The Effects Of Drugs And Alcohol

A sudden change in your body clock is not the only factor that can have a negative impact on your sleep patterns. The use of drugs, in particular, caffeine, alcohol, nicotine, and sleeping pills also has a negative impact on the quality of your sleep.

Caffeine

Caffeine is a potent stimulant related to amphetamines. It is found in many products including coffee, tea, chocolate and soft drinks. While caffeine's effects differ from person to person, you should generally avoid caffeinated products late in the evening. The caffeine in these products can cause difficulty in falling asleep and can cause you to wake up frequently during the night. You should be aware that the effects of caffeine peak about two to four hours after consumption.

Alcohol

Alcohol is classified as a depressant and any amount of use disturbs sleep patterns. Sleep researchers believe that alcohol suppresses REM sleep, and as a result, users spend less time in this important sleep stage. Alcohol causes people to wake up more often during the night and, as a result, they usually feel groggy in the morning.

 People may become *addicted* to alcohol. When this happens, *alcohol takes control of them!* Their lives revolve around getting the next drink and where they can hide their booze. Since you want to do your best and achieve your goals, *avoid alcohol!*

Nicotine

Nicotine (cigarettes) is also a stimulant that has effects similar to caffeine. Perry and Dawson note that heavy smokers have a harder time falling asleep and staying asleep. They also spend less time than non-smokers in deep and REM sleep. If you don't smoke, don't start! If you do smoke *quit*! Besides the obvious health benefits, quitting smoking will enable you to enjoy a higher quality of sleep.

Sleeping Pills

Sleep induced with sleeping pills results in an inferior quality of sleep. This type of sleep is lighter than normal sleep and results in less deep and REM sleep. This lack of quality sleep usually results in feeling tired when you wake up.

Summary

Your body functions on a cycle that determines when you should eat, be awake and sleep. When this cycle is disrupted, it can have a pronounced effect on your performance.

To be at your peak mentally, you must be at your peak physically. To maintain a high state of physical and mental readiness, keep your body's cycle as close to its normal routine as possible. Studying, taking examinations, and making presentations or speeches requires focus and concentration. Without adequate rest, such focus and concentration is not possible and you may jeopardize your performance even before you begin. Remember that drugs and alcohol can have a negative effect on your sleep cycle. When this happens, your mind will not be fully alert, and it will be difficult to put forth your best effort.

There are no limitations to the mind except those we acknowledge.

Napoleon Hill

The existence of forgetting has never been proved: we only know that some things don't come to mind when we want them.

Friedrich Nietzsche

Chapter Seven

THE MIND AND MEMORY:

THE STOREHOUSE
AND WORKHORSE OF KNOWLEDGE

What is the difference between the brain and the mind? How does the mind function? How does memory function? What is your capacity to remember? How can you remember more?

What Is The Mind?

Your brain is the *physical* organ in your head. The functions of the *mind* take place within the brain. While there is no clear, specific definition of the mind, it is believed to control all the functions of your being. Your mind is made up of your ability to think, reason, understand, determine right from wrong, and *remember*. This discussion focuses on memory, the ability of your mind to *remember*. Once you understand the capability and function of your mind and memory, you can begin to take advantage of your enormous hidden talent.

Understanding Memory

A reliable memory is essential for achievement in any field. Almost everyone has an opinion about their own memory. Some believe they have extraordinary memories. Others believe they have "bad" memories. What is the difference between these types of people? Is it a real or imagined difference? In fact, it is probably a combination of both.

People with "bad" memories, may not have a "bad" memory at all. A large part of memory depends on paying attention to what is to be learned or remembered. Imagine you are at a party. Someone introduces you to Ed Shedlock. When he says his name you may *hear* it, but do not *pay attention* to it. Later, when you speak to Mr. Shedlock again, you "forget" his name. Had you paid attention, it would have been a simple matter to remember Mr. Shedlock's name by associating his name with his face. Since he is partially bald, you could have told yourself, "That man has *shed* his *locks*," hence, Mr. Shedlock.

ED SHEDLOCK

This situation may reinforce a belief that one has a "bad" memory. However, you did not *forget* Ed Shedlock's name. You never *learned* it in the first place. So, a first step to improving your memory is to *pay attention* to what it is you want to learn or remember. When you *focus* your attention and *concentrate*, your memory will improve automatically. This is just as true for studying as it is for any other situation when instant recall is necessary.

There are three basic functions of your memory. Encoding or *labeling* information as you learn it; *storing* the information in your brain; and retrieving or *recalling* the information.

Labeling Information

In addition to paying attention, you can improve your memory by labeling the information you want to remember. This labeling process involves *associating* new information with information you *already know*, or *rearranging* it in a form to make remembering easier. To understand how labeling information can spell the difference between effective and ineffective recall, consider the following example.

Suppose you are a doctor. You have 100 patients and keep a file of information on each. However, you do not label each file, and you store all the files in a big box. A patient walks in with an emergency, and you need the patient's file immediately. Can you find it quickly to treat the patient properly? It is not likely. Now suppose each file is labeled clearly with each patient's name, and the files are placed in alphabetical order. Can you find it quickly? Of course you can.

Your memory functions very much in the same way. When you *label* information you want to learn, you can retrieve it *when you need it.* *Labeling* new information speeds up the search and retrieval process. For example, what are the colors of the rainbow? Did *ROY G. BIV* come to mind?

ROY stands for RED, ORANGE, YELLOW. G stands for GREEN and BIV stands for BLUE, INDIGO AND VIOLET. Using the first letter of each color to form a name (something with which you can associate) makes the colors easier to recall.

Memory aids like *ROY G. BIV* help you to *recall* information *when* you need it. The challenge to all students is to recall specific information at specific times and under specific time constraints. You can meet this challenge once you understand how to use memory aids. Using these aids to label information is explained and demonstrated further in Chapter 8.

Storing Information

Noted scholars believe that most people use less than ten per cent of their brain power, and that the potential of the brain to store new information is unlimited. Scientists and anthropologists believe the typical adult brain contains from fifteen to one hundred billion neurons. Each of these neurons holds a piece of information. Therefore, the capacity of your brain is unlimited, for all practical purposes. Your brain has the ability to store more information than you could ever care to learn!

To say a brain has fifteen to one hundred billion neurons is a difficult concept to understand. To get an idea just how great this range is, consider how large the number *one* billion is. How long do you think it would take to save one billion dollars ($1,000,000,000)? If you could save $1,000 a day, it would take about 3.3 years to save $1,000,000; however, it would take about 3,300 years to save one billion dollars!

Recalling Information

Recall is the process of retrieving stored information into your present thoughts. The more *frequently* you recall information, the more *firmly* it becomes *etched* in your memory. For example, you move and receive a new telephone number. For a short time you may not remember the number. However, over the next week or so, you have to look up or recall the number time and again to give it to your friends, family and acquaintances. Soon, you will not have to look up the number at all. Because you recalled the number often, it became etched in your memory. This analogy is especially true for academic information you must learn and remember. It is important to continually review new information: the review process builds strong memory traces.

Another point to understand is that memory by itself is not learning. However, memory assists in the learning process. Recalling new information frequently allows your mind the time it needs to assimilate and understand the information.

Cramming Is Not Learning

Have you ever waited until the last minute to study for an exam? If you have, you understand what a challenge it is to study and try to *remember* (not *learn*) a large amount of information in a small amount of time. It is not likely that real learning will take place when the intention is to repeat the information a short time later and then forget it.

 Cramming can be a frightening experience. When students cram, they cannot wait to get into the exam room and spill out the information as fast as they can. They are afraid of forgetting it. It may seem as though the information is slowly leaking out of their heads. The reason for this feeling is that the information occupies only a superficial image in memory.

You can equate cramming to blowing up a balloon that has a slow leak. As fast as the air goes in, it comes out. When you cram, the new information has no opportunity to make a lasting impression in your mind.

Summary

The functions and activities of the mind take place within the brain. No single portion of the brain can be identified as "the mind" because it does not have a physical presence, as does the brain. However, your mind controls all the functions of your being, including your ability to remember or your *memory*.

A reliable memory is essential for achievement in any field. The first step in establishing an effective memory is to *pay attention* to the information you desire to learn. You may believe you have a "bad" memory because you cannot remember names or faces. You probably do not forget names or faces: *you may not make the effort to learn them in the first place!*

Another step toward developing an effective memory is learning how to *label* information. *Labeling* involves associating *new* information with something you *already know*, or arranging it in a form that makes it easier to remember.

Storing information concerns the ability of the mind and brain to hold information. Although you may feel overwhelmed by all you need to remember, be assured the brain's potential to store new information is unlimited.

Recall is the process of retrieving information from storage into your present thoughts. The more *often you recall* stored information, the more *firmly* it will become *etched* in your mind. Simply stated, when you review study materials often, they will be easier to recall during a test.

Finally, cramming for exams is different from learning. Learning will not take place when the intention is to repeat the information quickly and then forget it. You are in school to *learn*! Keep up with your studies, review your materials as frequently as possible, and you will not have to cram.

If a task is once begun
Never leave it till it's done.
Be the labor great or small,
Do it well or not at all.

Unknown

Chapter Eight

MNEMONICS: MEMORY SYSTEMS

What in world is a mnemonic? How do you pronounce it?
How can a mnemonic make information easier to remember?

An Introduction To Mnemonics

Studying can be fun, interesting, and exciting when you use *mnemonics* (ne' mon iks). Simply stated, mnemonics are systems for labeling information. They are tools you can use to associate new information with something you already know (ROY G. BIV). Before explaining some different types of mnemonics, consider how a difficult assignment was turned into a *fun* and *easy* way to *remember* and *learn*. In this true situation, the mnemonic used was a song.

Kristen, daughter of co-author Tony Lipuma, was in the fifth grade. One day she came home from school complaining she had to memorize forty-nine prepositions for a test the following week. She gave her dad the list and said "Can you believe the teacher wants us to know these by next Tuesday? I don't know how I can do it." Dad glanced at the list and gave it back to her. Then he said "Look at the list." As she did, Dad began to sing thirty-seven of the forty-nine prepositions to the tune of the old time song "Swanee River." If you know the tune, try to sing along with the words. He sang:

> About above across after against
> Among around at before
> Behind below beneath between beyond
> By down during except
> For from in into near
> Of off on over out

Through throughout to toward under
Until up with without.

She was amazed. "How did you do that?" Kristen asked.
Dad explained that in the fifth grade he also had to learn the
prepositions, and the teacher taught them using music. (It was so
catchy, Dad retained the tune and words for thirty years!)

Once she learned the tune, she quickly memorized the
thirty-seven prepositions and made up her own way to remember
the remaining twelve. She had so much fun memorizing and
learning (prepositions have to be recognized as a part of speech)
that for several days she walked around the house singing the
song. While she did this, her six year-old sister, Lauren, picked
up the tune and now she also knows the words and tune. While
Lauren has *memorized*, she has not *learned*: she does not
understand that a preposition is a part of speech.

Kristen was so excited and enthusiastic that she told her
teacher about her unusual way of learning the prepositions. Her
teacher had her demonstrate the technique for the class. Several
schoolmates even called her, and she sang the preposition song to
them on the telephone.

The message in this story is that a challenging assignment
can be turned into a fun assignment and therefore made easier.
Isn't something easier when you *enjoy* doing it? Perhaps you do
not know the "Swanee River," but could you turn the preposition
song into another song you like? The challenge is yours, and

using your imagination and creativity will enhance your ability to *remember* and *learn*!

If you are not convinced of the value of mnemonics, take notice of a finding made by the U. S. Department of Education in its 1987 *What Works* study.

Research Finding: Memorizing can help students absorb and retain the factual information on which understanding and critical thought are based.

Comment: Most children at some time memorize multiplication tables, the correct spelling of words, historical dates, passages of literature such as the poetry of Robert Frost or the sonnets of Shakespeare. Memorizing *simplifies* the process of *recalling* information and allows its use to become automatic. Understanding and critical thought can then build on this base of knowledge and fact. Indeed, the more sophisticated mental operations of analysis, synthesis, and evaluation are *impossible* without *rapid* and *accurate recall* of bodies of specific knowledge.

Teachers can encourage students to develop memory skills by teaching highly structured and carefully sequenced lessons, with frequent reinforcement for correct answers. Young students, slow learners, and students who lack background knowledge can benefit from such instruction.

In addition, teachers can teach "mnemonics," that is, devices and techniques for improving memory. For example, the mnemonic "Every Good Boy Does Fine" has reminded generations of music students that E, G, B, D, and F are the notes to which the lines on a treble staff correspond. *Mnemonics* help students *remember* more information *faster* and *retain* it *longer*. *Comprehension and retention are even greater when teachers and students connect the new information being memorized with previous knowledge.*

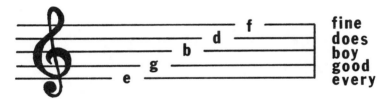

The following pages discuss some of the most popular and easy to use mnemonic systems. These systems also provide many versatile ways to make remembering easier. Please read and study about all the systems to understand how you can use these invaluable tools.

First Letter Mnemonics

First letter mnemonics are easy to construct, but like all mnemonics, require thought and imagination. You have already learned one of the most popular first letter mnemonics, ROY G. BIV. Now consider a few others.

Did you know that, when properly arranged, the first letters of each of the Great Lakes spells *HOMES*. The five Great Lakes are *H*uron, *O*ntario, *M*ichigan, *E*rie, and *S*uperior. Although, you have to remember each of the specific names, *HOMES* tells you the number of lakes and the first letter of each.

Did you know that the spaces in the treble clef spell *FACE*? Look at the clef and identify the note in each space.

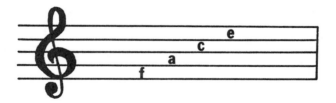

There is a first letter mnemonic for the four states in the United States that meet at a single point. The four states are *A*rizona, *U*tah, *C*olorado, and *N*ew Mexico. Use your imagination and arrange the first letter of each state to form a mnemonic. Did you arrange the letters to spell *CAN U* or *U CAN*? Armed with the first letter of each word and your imagination, you can always form some type of word or words.

Now examine what was a particularly difficult series to memorize. View such situations as a game or a challenge to be met, and your task becomes easier.

When Tony was studying for the CPA exam, he had to memorize a list of seventeen key words. He needed each word to develop a plan for conducting an audit. He tried several mnemonics before he chose R4IC3, FAVE POST. There were 4 "R" words (*read*, *recite*, *review*, *recalculate*), hence *R4*; 3 "I" words, (*inspect*, *inquire*, *interrelate*), and 3 "C" words, *compare*, *confirm*, *count*), hence *IC3*; and the first letters of the last eight words spelled *FAVE POST* (*foot*, *analyze*, *vouch*, *examine*, *prove*, *observe*, *scan* and *trace*). As Tony did, make up words like *FAVE* if necessary. He believes this mnemonic proved to be an invaluable tool for remembering this information.

Acrostic Mnemonics

Remember "Every Good Boy Does Fine?" This is an example of an acrostic. An acrostic is a series of words using the first letter of each item to be remembered. What are the names of the planets in the solar system starting with the one closest to the sun? They are: *M*ercury, *V*enus, *E*arth, *M*ars, *J*upiter, *S*aturn, *U*ranus, *N*eptune, and *P*luto. In one book explaining memory techniques, an acrostic was developed to remember the planets: *M*y *V*ery *E*xcellent *M*other *J*ust *S*erved *U*s *N*ine *P*ickles. As you can see again, the first letter of each word corresponds to the first letter of each planet in order.

**MY VERY EXCELLENT MOTHER
JUST SERVED US NINE PICKLES**

Here is an acrostic for remembering the steps in researching a tax question. *"Old Dirty Ladies Eat Dogs and Cats."* This mnemonic stands for (1) *O*btain the facts, (2) *D*escribe the problem, (3) *L*ocate the authority, (4) *E*valuate the authority, (5) *D*erive the solution, and (6) *C*ommunicate the answer. Mnemonics that are outrageous or humorous, such as this one, are easier to remember when they can be vividly pictured in your mind.

Rhyme Mnemonics

Using your imagination, you can create rhymes to remember needed information. How can you remember the year in which Columbus discovered America?

In 1492, Columbus sailed the ocean blue.

How do you remember which months have thirty or thirty-one days?

Thirty days have September
April, June and November.
All the rest have thirty-one
Except February which has twenty-eight.

How can you remember the fate of the six wives of Henry the Eighth?

> Divorced, Beheaded, Died
> Divorced, Beheaded, Survived.

Once you memorize a rhyme, you will remember it for a long time.

Song and Tune Mnemonics

One sure way to remember information quickly and easily is to turn it into a song. This was the secret of the preposition song. How often do you catch yourself singing songs or jingles from commercials? You probably have even caught yourself singing tunes you did not like. Have you noticed what happens when you hear an old song? You can immediately pick up the words and tune again.

You have heard some tunes so many times they are locked in your mind. You could not forget them if you wanted to. One of the authors remembered the entire preposition song for thirty years! To the extent it is practical, use music as a device to retain and recall needed information.

Pegword Mnemonics

The principle behind using pegword mnemonics is to associate a series of words or pegs with information you want to learn. For a series of ten items, think of a word that rhymes with the numbers one to ten. Each rhyming word should be a noun that can be visualized distinctly. Try the following rhyming words with the numbers one to ten: one-sun, two-shoe, three-tree, four-door, five-hive, six-sticks, seven-heaven, eight-gate, nine-sign, ten-pen. Each word connected with the numbers one through ten is the pegword. Review the numbers and the corresponding rhyming words (pegwords) until you feel comfortable that you know them. Clearly picture each pegword in your mind. You can use these rhyming or pegwords anytime you want to remember a list of ten items.

Recall that each pegword is a concrete noun, something that can be visualized. *Visualizing* each pegword is vital to the success of this system. Before you try using the peg system, read the following list of ten items: (1) book, (2) house, (3) train, (4) airplane, (5) desk, (6) clock, (7) picture, (8) map, (9) box, (10) umbrella. Read the list again and try to write down the items from memory. Record the number correct.

Now, use the peg system to match the pegwords with the ten items: one-sun-book, two-shoe-house, three-tree-train, four-door-airplane, five-hive-desk, six-sticks-clock, seven-heaven-picture, eight-gate-map, nine-sign-box, ten-pen-umbrella. Try the following exercise. Read each item only long enough to make the visualization.

First, see the *sun* brightly shining on a giant *book* in front of your house. The book is open and the glare off the pages is blinding. Second, see a *house* (a specific house, yours or even the White House) full of *shoes*, from top to bottom. Third, see a *train* locomotive sitting in a *tree*. Fourth, imagine a *door* with an *airplane* stuck in the opening. Fifth, see your *desk*, at school or work, with a bee *hive* on it, and bees swarming all around. Sixth, imagine a giant *clock* supported by *sticks*. Seventh, imagine a devil in a *picture* with the title "*Heaven.*" Eighth, open a *gate* that you know of and see a *map* of the United States lying on the ground. Ninth, imagine driving on a highway where all the *signs* are displayed on *box*es. Tenth, see yourself using the handle in an open *umbrella* as a *pen*.

Now recall the list and notice your improvement. Using the pegwords and visualizing the associations has increased your ability to remember.

Try the same exercise with the lists on page 104, and make up your own visualizations. Again, read each list twice and try to recall as many items as you can. Then, use the pegwords and the visualization process only spending enough time on each item to "see a picture." Try to make your visualizations funny or even ridiculous. Finally, recall the list and notice your improvement when you used the pegword system.

FIVE-HIVE-DESK

LIST 1	LIST 2	LIST 3	LIST 4
car	boat	dog	cat
television	bear	suitcase	jacket
paper	teacher	ticket	pencil
book	lamp	chair	rose
teabag	rug	glass	table
bird	telephone	computer	jar
envelope	box	shirt	cloud
saw	grass	water	hammer
roof	basket	letter	wheel
briefcase	pillow	paint	radio

The Loci System

The loci (lo si) system may be the oldest mnemonic system. It was used by the ancient Greeks and Romans. The system is easy to learn and it uses places and locations to remember information. The system can be used to remember any type of information and is particularly useful when giving speeches.

It works like this. Select a place or location for your loci. It can be your home, school or place of work. The trick is to *visualize* yourself taking a tour of your loci and *finding* one or more pieces of information at each stop along the tour.

Suppose you are to deliver a speech on the value of mnemonics in the learning process. You want to be certain to discuss all the important mnemonic systems. How can you use the loci system to help you remember each system? Use your home as the loci.

Visualize yourself arriving at home and walking toward the front door. As you approach the door, you see a series of individual letters (A, B, C, etc.) pinned to it. This reminds you of the first letter system. You next walk into the house and go to the kitchen, where you see a pegboard (peg system) with a note taped to it. The note says "Every good boy does fine," (acrostic). You now move to the refrigerator to get a drink. Taped to the door you see a favorite poem (rhyme). You can go on with such a tour until you have placed all the mnemonic systems in different places in the house.

This system is valuable because it provides an organized method to recall needed information in the sequence you want to remember it. Like other mnemonic systems, the loci system has value outside the learning environment. You can use it to help you to remember any type of information.

You can use several loci to remember different sets of information. For example, you can use school as a loci to remember school related information, or your place of work to remember work related information.

The Phonetic/Number
Alphabet System

One of the most useful and versatile mnemonic systems is the phonetic number/alphabet system. However, the system is complex and is beyond the intended scope of this book. The system associates consonant sounds with the numbers zero through nine. The sounds are combined with vowels to turn numbers, dates, etc., into words, which are easier to remember. To learn about this system, read Harry Lorayne's book, *Super Memory - Super Student* and Kenneth L. Higbee's book *Your Memory - How It Works and How To Improve It.* Your patience and perseverance will be rewarded when you learn the unlimited uses for this system.

Miscellaneous Mnemonics

You have been introduced to several recognized mnemonic systems. You can also make up your own types of mnemonics. Remember, mnemonics are based on associations and anything that assists memory is a mnemonic. So, be creative and use what works best for you.

Suppose you must remember the United States entered World War II in 1941. You are nineteen years old and your dad happens to be forty-one. Use the association of your ages to remember the year. Associate the months and days of birthdays, anniversaries, and other important dates with information you must learn. Make up silly and crazy associations if necessary. When one student had difficulty remembering riboflavin (a component of Vitamin B), he made up the phrase "rib off Alaskan."

Here are a few others to demonstrate the unlimited possibilities. You can remember that a dromedary camel has one hump, as in a capital D. A bactrain camel two humps, as in a capital B. A stala*c*tite is formed from the *c*eiling, and a stala*g*mite is formed from the *g*round.

To remember a numerical formula, try turning the numbers into words. How can you remember that Pi = 3.1416? You can remember this by turning the formula into *Yes, I have a castle*. "*Yes*" has three letters, "*I*" has one, "*have*" has four, "*a*" has one and "*castle*" has six.

Summary

Mnemonics are memory aids. They are techniques for labeling information to make recall easier. Mnemonics help to make learning fun and interesting.

First letter mnemonics use the first letter of a series of words to form a single word. *HOMES* is a first letter mnemonic for the Great Lakes (Huron, Ontario, Michigan, Erie and Superior). Acrostic mnemonics use the first letter of each word to form a sentence or phrase. *M*y *V*ery *E*xcellent *M*other *J*ust *S*erved *U*s *N*ine *P*ickles, is an acrostic for the planets in our solar

A **B**ACTRAIN AND A **D**ROMEDARY CAMEL

system by distance from the sun (*M*ercury, *V*enus, *E*arth, *M*ars, *J*upiter, *S*aturn, *U*ranus, *N*eptune, and *P*luto).

Rhyme mnemonics use rhymes to make remembering easier. A well known rhyme mnemonic is "In 1492, Columbus sailed the ocean blue." You can use music to set information to a catchy song or tune. Songs and jingles can be remembered for years.

Pegword mnemonics associate a series or list of words with "pegwords" tied to the numbers one to ten. The system relies on visualizations to be effective. The loci system uses a "location" to "place" information you want to remember. You can mentally take a systematic tour of your home to "find" information you have "placed" in different parts of the house.

It should be apparent there is no limit to the types of mnemonics you can create. You need only call upon the imagination and creativity within you. Remember, the most effective mnemonics are those that are *visual, silly, absurd* and *ridiculous*. These types of mental pictures form lasting impressions. It should also be obvious that mnemonics have applications far beyond an academic setting. They can be used to remember names, faces, grocery lists, chores, and anything else you can imagine. Start remembering more effectively today, and *enjoy* doing it!

*You never know
until you try.
And you never try
unless you <u>really</u> try.
You give it your best shot;
you do the best you can.*

*And if you've done everything
in your power, and still "fail"-
the truth of the matter is
that you haven't failed at all.*

*When you reach for your dreams,
no matter what they may be,
you grow from the reaching;
you learn from the trying;
you win from the doing.*

Laine Parsons

SECTION III:
THE MASTER STUDENT

USING STRATEGIES AND SKILLS TO EXCEL

Congratulations! You are on the final leg of your journey. Soon you will be *THE MASTER STUDENT*. You have developed the desire to achieve and understand that your potential is far beyond what you thought was possible. You have learned you can be what you want to be!

Now, you must learn to apply specific study strategies and skills to ensure each day is successful. Remember the new definition of success? Once you begin to do your best each day, you will achieve the grades you desire and *deserve*!

Academics was compared to athletics at the beginning of the book. At this stage, it is important to recall this relationship. By understanding how athletes reach their goals through dedication, persistence, and practice, you can relate this understanding to reaching your academic goals.

A student preparing for an examination or series of examinations is akin to an athlete preparing for a competition. Think of preparing for a major exam as preparing for the mental olympics.

An athlete must train continuously to maintain peak performance. The athlete practices again and again, usually in the same environment. The student, too, must work continuously, but must choose the best environment in which to train (for example, your home, or the library). Like the athlete, the student must develop a consistent program and follow that program to reach his or her goal.

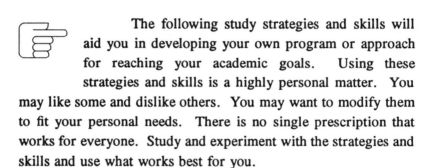 The following study strategies and skills will aid you in developing your own program or approach for reaching your academic goals. Using these strategies and skills is a highly personal matter. You may like some and dislike others. You may want to modify them to fit your personal needs. There is no single prescription that works for everyone. Study and experiment with the strategies and skills and use what works best for you.

When things go wrong, as they sometimes will,
When the road you're trudging seems all up hill,
When the funds are low and the debts are high,
And you want to smile, but you have to sigh,
When care is pressing you down a bit,
Rest, if you must-but don't you quit.

Life is queer with its twists and turns,
As everyone of us sometimes learns,
And many a failure turns about
When he might have won had he stuck it out;
Don't give up, though the pace seems slow--
You might succeed with another blow.

Often the goal is nearer than
It seems to a faint and faltering man,
Often the struggler has given up
When he might have captured the victor's cup.
And he learned too late, when the night slipped down,
How close he was to the golden crown.

Success is failure turned inside out-
The silver tint of the clouds in doubt-
And you never can tell how close you are,
It may be near when it seems afar;
So stick to the fight when you're hardest hit-
It's when things seems worst that you mustn't quit.

Unknown

Chapter Nine

STUDY STRATEGIES:

A PLAN OF ATTACK

What are study strategies? How can study strategies result in better grades? Do they really work?

Develop The Ability To Relax

Can you recall an experience when you tried very hard to remember something? It may have seemed as though the information was on the "tip of your tongue," but you could not remember it. The harder you tried to remember, the more difficult it became. When did you finally recall the information? It probably came to you at a time when you were not actively and deliberately trying to recall it. In other words, it came to you when your mind was relaxed.

A certain level of stress can help to get your thinking faculties into high gear. However, once you exceed this level, it may become difficult to think clearly and recall information. This is precisely what can happen on an examination when your mind "seems to go blank."

Besides affecting your recall ability, stress can affect your ability to learn new information. For example, suppose you attempt to begin a study session and feel tense and upset as a result of an argument or other stressful situation. Under these conditions, your ability to study effectively will be impaired. You will probably continue to relive the recent events, and you will not concentrate or focus on the material at hand.

Learning comes more naturally and with less effort when you are relaxed: your mind is clearer and has an increased ability to take in and retain new information.

There are several ways to deal with the effects of stress and its negative influence on your ability to learn. Physical exercise, yoga and meditation are all excellent techniques to control stress and induce relaxation. There are also simple relaxation techniques you can learn and practice on your own. Try the following exercise before beginning a study session.

Relaxation Exercise:
A Study Situation

The objective of the exercise is to completely relax your body and clear your mind. The exercise is intended to be effortless. You are in effect, putting your mind in a shutdown mode, you are giving it a complete rest. Read the following instructions and then practice this relaxation exercise.

1. Find a quiet room with soft lighting.

2. Sit up straight in a comfortable chair. Let your arms hang at your sides and close your eyes. Take your glasses off if you wear them.

3. Take several deep breaths, breathing in through your nose and out through your mouth. Then, breathe at a leisurely pace.

4. Feel all the muscles in your body go limp. Start with your facial muscles, then your neck and

shoulders. Feel your arms, legs, and feet become limp and completely relaxed.

5.   Choose a soothing word such as "relax" or "peaceful." Choose any word that suggests a state of relaxation or peace of mind. Continually repeat the word to yourself. Say the word slowly and feel yourself entering a state of deep relaxation as you say it. Peaceful. Peaceful. The sound of the word itself is relaxing.

6.   Keep saying the word to yourself but do not try to keep your mind focused on the word. Your mind will wander and this is natural. When you become aware that your word is no longer in your thoughts, again repeat it to yourself. Again allow your mind to drift. Although you are directing your mind to the "word," you are not forcing your mind to concentrate on it. Can you feel the stress and tension being released from your mind and body?

7.   Try to remain in this relaxed state for at east five to ten minutes. As you become more proficient, try extending the time to fifteen and then to twenty minutes.

8.   At the end of your session, take a minute or so to take a few deep breaths and get up slowly. Do not try to go from a completely relaxed state to an

active state by jumping up when your session is completed.

Try to make this exercise a part of your study routine. You will be amazed at the positive results it produces.

Do Your Homework

Whenever a teacher gives you a routine assignment that must be turned in, complete the assignment on time and in a neat and legible fashion. This type of behavior lets your teacher know you are a serious student and that you produce quality work. Teachers from elementary school to college either grade homework assignments or track the number of assignments completed (yes, even some college professors). This process helps them to determine the effort put forth by a student. A student's level of effort can spell the difference between receiving an *A* or *B*.

Suppose you are the teacher. You have two students with high *B* averages. One student has adequately completed all assignments on time. The other student completed about seventy-five per cent of the assignments and several were turned in late. Would you consider giving the first student an *A*? How about the second student? You can see that while both students have the same grade, the student who worked harder is more likely to be rewarded for his or her efforts.

Establish A Schedule

Establishing a schedule to complete your daily and longer term tasks is essential to achieving the results you want. Schedules are a tool to use and modify as needed. They are not intended to limit your flexibility and creativity.

Schedules organize your life, help you to use your time effectively, enable you to see your accomplishments, and allow you to *enjoy* your leisure activities more fully. While you do not have to become a "schedule slave," you must have a plan of attack. Someone once correctly observed, "If you fail to plan, you plan to fail."

Without a schedule, you can become frustrated and confused. When you set priorities, it is easier to accomplish what needs to be done. Haven't you found this to be true? Remember when you had term papers due, and one or more major examinations within a two week period? Although you were aware of the due dates at the beginning of the term, you did not establish a plan to finish each project and study for each exam. Then, you went crazy trying to decide which to do first to complete all tasks on time!

Creating A Routine Study Schedule

The first step in establishing a schedule is to determine how you presently spend your time. Using Exhibit 9.1 (high school) or Exhibit 9.2 (college), chart how you think you spend your time for a typical week. First, start with the time you wake up (which may not be the same every day), and then fill in the times for your commitments that do not change from week to week. Include time for getting ready for school or work, class times, and meal times. This is your "fixed" schedule. Next, fill in the time you *think* you spend for studying, school projects, recreation and leisure.

Your next task is to chart your actual daily activities for about a week. Again using Exhibit 9.1 or 9.2, chart the *actual* time spent for each activity. You may be surprised at what you find. How much actual time did you spend studying or working on school projects? Do not include the time you were interrupted by a telephone call, got a snack, or took a half hour break to watch a television show. Did you spend as much time as you thought? It is easy to delude yourself into believing you studied for an adequate period, when your time was interrupted by other activities.

When you have seen in writing how you spend your time (as opposed to guessing how it is spent), construct a study schedule for specific times on specific days. Be realistic. Although it can be changed, make up a schedule you can stick to.

Establishing a routine may seem difficult at first because you are not accustomed to it. However, recall that it usually takes about twenty-one days to form new habits. After establishing a schedule, try it for about three weeks and decide if it suits your needs.

	MON	TUE	WED	THR	FRI	SAT	SUN
7-8	BREAKFAST and GET READY ⟶						
8-9	⟵ English ⟶					BREAK-FAST	
9-10	⟵ Math ⟶						BREAK-FAST
10-11	⟵ Science ⟶						
11-12	LUNCH ⟶						
12-1	⟵ Spanish ⟶						
1-2	⟵ Phys. Ed. ⟶						
2-3	⟵ History ⟶						
3-4							
4-5							
5-6							
6-7	DINNER ⟶						
7-8							
8-9							
9-10							
10-11							
11-12	SLEEP ⟶						

Exhibit 9.1

	MON	TUE	WED	THR	FRI	SAT	SUN
7·8	BREAKFAST and GET READY ⟶						
8·9	English		English		English	BREAK-FAST	
9·10		Statistics		Statistics			BREAK-FAST
10·11							
11·12	History		History		History		
12·1	LUNCH ─────────────────────⟶						
1·2		Biology		Biology LAB			
2·3							
3·4	Photo-graphy		Photo-graphy	↓	Photo-graphy LAB		
4·5							
5·6					↓		
6·7	DINNER ────────────────────⟶						
7·8							
8·9							
9·10							
10·11							
11·12	SLEEP ────────────────⟶						

Exhibit 9.2

Creating Weekly, Monthly
and Term Schedules

You need a schedule to help you (1) get assignments completed on time, and (2) complete studying and reviewing material before an exam. Consider purchasing a calendar or appointment book that contains all the months of the year and a block for each day of the month. As an alternative, you can purchase calendar sheets similar to those shown in Exhibit 9.3. You can use these monthly type calendars to track short and long-term assignments simultaneously. If you have a personal computer, you can purchase inexpensive software to create your own weekly or monthly calendars.

It is important to see an entire month on one page. Seeing a whole month helps you to assess the relative importance of one assignment or exam against another. Use as many monthly calendars as you need for each month of the term.

Short-Term Assignments

Short-term assignments are easy to deal with since they are of short duration, i.e., an assignment due within two weeks. You might get a reading assignment on Monday that is due Friday. Or, you might be told that next Wednesday there will be a quiz on four chapters. Put these items on your schedule, and track them for the short time until completion. Take note: to fit unexpected short-term assignments into your schedule, you may have to rearrange some priorities.

Long-Term Assignments

The situation is much different for long-term assignments. At the beginning of the term, immediately record all long-term assignments and scheduled exams on the calendar. Record subsequent ones as you become aware of them.

To schedule completion of a long-term assignment or preparation for an exam, you must select several intermediate dates to complete segments of your assignment or review process. Suppose you have a mid-term exam on October 30 that covers the first eight chapters of your book (see Exhibit 9.3). Your teacher may continue to teach new material until one or two classes before the exam. Therefore, you cannot afford to wait until the teacher completes all the material to begin studying. You must plan for time to review all the preceding chapters so that, just before the exam, you will only have to cover one or two new chapters. To prepare such a plan, your schedule should show when (the dates before October 30) you will complete your review of each chapter.

Planning to complete a term paper or other project is similar to planning an exam review. You must decide when to complete stages of the project to remain on track for the due date. If you have three months to develop a topic and prepare a paper, you might decide that by the end of the second week you will select a topic. By the end of the sixth week, you will complete your research. By the end of the eighth week you will complete the first draft, and by the end of the tenth week you will produce a final report. Put each intermediate completion date on your calendar. This schedule will enable you to complete the process about two weeks ahead of schedule!

When you are given a long-term assignment such as a term paper, begin to consider a topic immediately. The sooner you select a topic, the sooner your mind can begin to develop ideas for the paper. As these ideas come to you, write them down. You may be surprised at the number of different ideas you can consider.

Study Exhibits 9.3 and 9.4 to understand how to complete a review for the mid-term exam and the paper due three weeks before the end of the term. The periodic review shown for the exam will not take long. Follow this process. By doing so, you will thoroughly understand and have effective recall of the material learned.

 Once you begin scheduling and meeting the intermediate dates, you will discover that it is easier to complete a project when you plan properly. As you complete each assignment or intermediate step, cross it off your calendar so you can track your progress. This crossing off process provides a feeling of achievement and satisfaction for the work completed. So often people (not just students) believe they work hard toward a goal, but become frustrated because they cannot see their progress. Recording assignments and noting their

S	**SUN**	**MON**	**TUE**	**WED**	**THR**	**FRI**	**SAT**
E	1	2	3 *SCHOOL BEGINS*	4	5	6	7
P	8	9	10	11	12	13	14 *PAPER- select Topic*
T							
E	15 *Exam Review Chapters 1-2*	16	17	18	19	20	21
M							
B	22	23	24	25	26	27	28
E							
R	29 *Exam Review 1-4*	30					

SUN	**MON**	**TUE**	**WED**	**THR**	**FRI**	**SAT**	
		1	2	3	4	5	**O**
6	7	8	9	10	11	12 *PAPER- Finish Research*	**C**
13 *Exam Review 1-6*	14	15	16	17	18	19	**T**
20 *Exam Review 1-7*	21	22	23	24	25	26 *PAPER- 1st Draft*	**O**
27 *Exam Review 1-8*	28	29	30 *MID TERM EXAM*	31			**B**
							E
							R

Exhibit 9.3

127

N O V E M B E R

SUN	MON	TUE	WED	THR	FRI	SAT
					1	2
3	4	5	6	7	8	9 *PAPER- Finish Revisions*
10	11	12	13	14	15	16 *PAPER- FINAL*
17	18	19	20	21	22	23
24	25	26	27	28	29	30

SUN	MON	TUE	WED	THR	FRI	SAT
1	2 *HISTORY PAPER DUE*	3	4	5	6	7
8	9	10	11	12	13	14
15	16	17	18	19	20 *END of TERM*	21
22	23	24	25	26	27	28
29	30	31				

D E C E M B E R

Exhibit 9.4

completion provides the feedback you *need* to continue the path toward reaching a goal (completing assignments and exams).

Other Benefits Of A Schedule

Think of the peace of mind you can enjoy knowing you have a plan to complete your assignments on time. Even if your schedule begins to slip for a day or so (and at some point it will), you can adjust and fine tune your plan to stay on target. Using a schedule will keep you from being overwhelmed by your assignments and examinations. Instead of having to juggle a vague schedule in your mind, you will always see what you have accomplished and what lies ahead.

By using your schedule, you will manage your time effectively, and you will enjoy your leisure time even more. If you are a football fan, can you relate to what it is like to watch a football game Sunday afternoon when you know you should be studying? Although you are trying to enjoy the game, a black cloud hangs over your head because you know you should be studying instead of watching the game. If, however, you use a schedule, you can plan to have your work done before the game, and then enjoy the rest of the day.

Establish A Set Place To Study

It is important to set a specific place for studying. By doing so, you can establish a routine and feel comfortable in your "study place." You will associate this place with studying and learning. You can study in your room, the kitchen, living room, dining room, the library or at a friend's house. It should be a place you can use on a regular basis.

If you study in your room, you might not want to associate your room exclusively with studying. You can, however, designate specific times in your room as the study period. You can then associate your room as the "study place" during these times.

When you study, make sure there is adequate lighting. Proper lighting will help to ensure (1) you do not suffer from eye strain, and (2) you do not fall asleep. Use two lamps, if possible, with 100 watt bulbs in each. As an alternative, try to find a place with adequate overhead lighting and consider using a high intensity desk lamp.

You should make a habit of sitting in a chair when studying. Sit upright and avoid slouching. Sitting with good posture benefits you physically as well as helping you to remain alert.

Imagine trying to study in your room, on your bed, with inadequate lighting. Honestly now, *will that work*? You are trying to study a subject you do not find interesting. You try sitting with your legs crossed for a while, but this position does not last long because your back starts to hurt. Next, you try stretching out on your stomach with the book in front of you. Now, your neck and back hurts. You try lying on your back and holding the book over your head in front of your face. Now your arms get tired. All the while you never had proper lighting on the reading material and, as a result, your eyes are getting tired. Does this situation sound familiar?

If you can survive this ordeal for an hour, you are lucky. But how efficient or effective was this study session? You were constantly moving around and continually disrupting your concentration. You probably did not focus on any issue long enough to grasp its meaning completely. You, therefore, did not understand the material as well as you should have, and you will have to spend more time studying this material later. This whole scenario also assumes that you did not fall asleep within the first ten to fifteen minutes after beginning.

Talk to some students that consistently get good grades. Find out how they study, and you will understand that your grades are related to your study habits.

Avoid Distractions

Your study environment should be quiet and free of distractions. You do not want to study within earshot of a television, radio, someone's conversation, or other background noise. Too often, you are drawn to listen to such distractions.

When this happens, you break your concentration and focus. Concentration requires directed mental effort. You cannot *effectively* focus on two subjects at the same time. Imagine you are in the kitchen trying to study a mathematical formula. The television is blasting from the living room, and you are listening to the program as you study. Since television programs are easy to understand, you may follow the plot, but you will not understand and learn the math formula. Your attention will constantly shift back and forth from the television to math. As a result, you will not understand the formula and must spend additional time studying. You will have wasted valuable time.

Not everyone has the opportunity to study under ideal conditions, that is, without background distractions. If this is the case, you will need extra dedication, focus, and concentration to block out the distractions and do your work.

Do you recall the discussion about your ability to remember? The first rule of effective memory or recall is to *pay attention*! It is difficult to learn anything when you do not pay attention to it in the first place.

Avoid Interruptions

When you begin studying, be determined not to be interrupted. To avoid interruptions, *have all your study materials on-hand*. Then, you will not have to go somewhere else to get your calculator, pencils, books, or reference materials. If you are missing a needed item, try to wait until you reach a pre-established break time.

Avoid making or taking telephone calls during study periods. Unless it is absolutely necessary to obtain help or clarification from a friend, do not make or receive disrupting calls. Every time something disrupts your focus, it takes additional time to get back to where you were.

You may view these suggestions as too harsh or regimented because you are not in the habit of studying efficiently and effectively. Studying *efficiently* means making the best use of your available study time (concentrating and avoiding distractions). Studying *effectively*, means getting the results you want. These results include learning (not just reading information) and demonstrating your depth of knowledge on an examination.

When you learn to study efficiently and effectively you will *discover* (yes, discover) that you will (1) spend *less* time studying, (2) *learn* and *absorb* more information, and (3) spend less time *worrying* about your grades because you will be getting the grades you want!

Develop An Interest
In Your Subject

It is difficult to study a subject in which you have little interest. It seems to require all the effort you can muster. Furthermore, the actual degree of learning is less than it would be if you had an interest in the subject.

Imagine studying something in which you already have a keen interest. Assume that you are interested in tennis, fishing, or needlepoint. Because your interest level is high, the information seems easy to comprehend and you retain most of what you read. Learning is easy and comes more naturally because you *enjoy* what you are learning.

It is possible to develop an interest in any subject when you relate it to something you know already, or something you might want to know in the future. Take geometry as an example. What is the point of learning all those formulas? Why is it necessary to know the formula for the area of a rectangle, the circumference of a circle, or the hypotenuse of a right triangle?

Why? Because this information can be useful now or later in life. Suppose you want to buy carpet for your living room. How could you possibly compute the number of square yards to buy if you do not know the formula for the area of a rectangle?

Another subject that might appear to be uninteresting is English grammar and composition. English is pretty boring, isn't it? No! Although your teachers might not tell you directly, the purpose of this subject is to teach you to communicate properly and effectively. Effectively here means getting another person to understand your ideas, or being able to persuade someone to understand (not necessarily accept) your point of view. Effective communication is the basis for all interaction among people!

You should now understand that the purpose of english grammar and composition goes beyond establishing a set of rules just to aggravate you. Can you now develop *some* interest in this subject?

Abraham Lincoln had only one year of formal education, yet he spent many years reading literary classics including Shakespeare and the Bible. Through this effort, he learned to use language to communicate his ideas and feelings in a clear and concise manner. Today, Lincoln is regarded as one of the most effective communicators of all time. If you doubt this fact, read his Gettysburg Address! Even Lincoln underestimated himself when he said, "The world will little note, nor long remember, what we say here . . . ." His Gettysburg Address has become one of the most famous speeches of all time.

Study In Short Bursts

It is more effective to divide a study session into several shorter periods, with breaks between them, than it is to study straight for an hour or more. Each study period should be about thirty minutes in length. There are several reasons to explain this finding.

When you study for an hour or more without a break, your concentration and focus will drift. Haven't you found this to be true? On the other hand, you probably found that you do not have a problem maintaining your focus for about thirty minutes at a time. When you remain focused for the entire thirty minutes, you learn and retain more.

There is another reason for breaking up a long study period. You tend to remember the most about the first and last topics covered during a study session. Suppose you intend to study for ninety minutes. By breaking up this study period into three separate periods, you automatically triple the number of beginning and ending study periods. In this way, you can retain three times as much information. Review Exhibit 9.5 to see the difference between a solid ninety minute session, and three separate sessions totalling ninety minutes. Each *1* represents a beginning, and a *2* represents an ending of a study period.

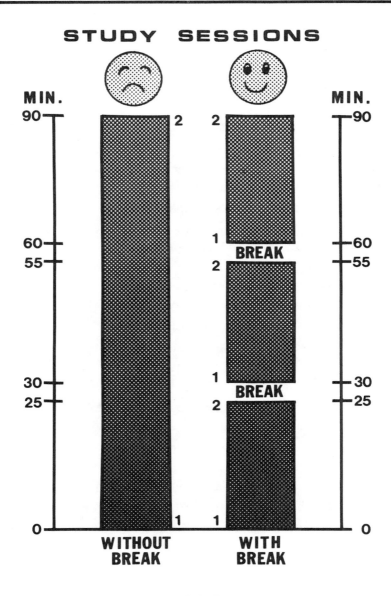

Exhibit 9.5

Plan Each Study Session

Decide in advance what topics within each subject you will cover. Decide what you expect to learn from each session. *Study with a purpose!*

Suppose a teacher has lectured on the events that led to the drafting and signing of the Declaration of Independence. The teacher has now assigned a reading. Obviously this reading or chapter has a topic. What additional knowledge do you intend to gain from reading the material? Knowing what you intend to learn will keep you interested in your work.

Decide how much material you will cover. Your task will be easier when you define what you plan to accomplish, in effect setting a goal for each session. Suppose you are assigned to read a thirty page chapter. Will you read all thirty pages in this session, or  only fifteen? Once you decide, place a marker at the page where you plan to stop. Then, you can always see how far you have to go.

How often have you disrupted your concentration by counting the number of pages left? Once you lose your focus, it may take several minutes to reacquaint yourself with the information you were studying.

Use Available Time Effectively

The purpose of this section is to explain how to make productive use of "down time" during a typical day. You do not have to become a study machine that never rests. On the contrary, if you turn unproductive time into productive time, you will have more opportunities for other activities.

How do you spend your time when you are waiting to see the doctor or dentist? You probably spend a lot of time waiting. Instead of staring at the ceiling, reading a magazine you do not like, or wondering why everyone else is there, how about reading one of your assignments? Remember about studying in short bursts? Well, this is a perfect opportunity. Do not get caught up in the false belief that you must have at least an hour to accomplish anything of significance. Every study period helps, and a series of short study periods builds into knowledge.

Waiting for the doctor or dentist is just one example of planning to use available time. How about when you are waiting for your car to be repaired or when you are waiting in line for *hours* to buy concert tickets? Surely you can accomplish something worthwhile during those time periods.

For those of you who commute to school or work, use your commuting time to better advantage. Perhaps it sounds strange, but the time spent commuting to and from work or school can be productive. You can dictate your notes or summaries onto cassettes and listen to the tapes during your commute. You can then take advantage of this time to reinforce your understanding and knowledge of the particular subject!

You also invested a fair amount of your time reading and learning about how your mind and body function in the first two sections of this book. There are many excellent instructional and motivational programs on cassette. These programs help to keep you on your set course by providing new and exciting insights into human thought and behavior. You can listen to these programs in total privacy whether you are in your car or listening to your "Walkman" on the subway.

Avoid Interference

No, this is not the same topic as interruptions. Interference is created when you study two similar subjects back-to-back *within the same study session*. When this happens, you may confuse one topic with another.

There may be times in your educational career when you will take two similar courses at the same time. For example, you might take French and Spanish, world history and United States history, or biology and chemistry. You should not study Spanish immediately after studying French, or biology immediately after chemistry. Since the subjects do have some common ground, you might begin to confuse what you learned in one subject with the other. A better way to approach this situation would be to study the subjects in the following order: Spanish, biology, and then

French. Or, you might study biology, French, and then chemistry.

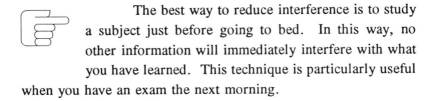 The best way to reduce interference is to study a subject just before going to bed. In this way, no other information will immediately interfere with what you have learned. This technique is particularly useful when you have an exam the next morning.

Join Study Groups

Study groups can make a real difference in your level of understanding. This increased understanding will result in better exam performance. Law students have traditionally used study groups to increase their knowledge and understanding of a subject.

Study groups can function in any manner the participants desire. You can meet to discuss specific topics, or each group member can be assigned a topic on which to report to the group. In this way, not every group member has to spend his or her time performing the same tasks.

A study group increases your understanding of a topic because you must actively *listen and evaluate* the ideas of other students. Not every student has the same level of comprehension of each topic. By discussing the topics in a group, each student has an opportunity to ask questions and to gain the same level of understanding as the other participants.

There is another invaluable benefit to participating in a study group. As you discuss each topic, you are making additional memory traces of the subject. Your retention and understanding of the subject increase because you use several senses to process information. First, you *listen* to others and *see* them provide explanations simultaneously. If the discussion becomes lively, all the better. Recall that you remember better when you put emotion into your work. Second, after you mentally evaluate what you have heard, you provide your assessment by *speaking* to the group. When you *hear* yourself provide this evaluation, it further strengthens your memory traces.

Many students are reluctant to initiate a study group. If this is the case, look for an opportunity when you can casually approach the subject with fellow students. A perfect time is when students are informally discussing a subject before or after class. If the subject is particularly interesting, notice how animated and enthusiastic the participants seem. They may not admit it, but they are *enjoying* the experience of sharing and debating their ideas with other people.

Take Advantage Of The "Real World"

A tremendously effective way to learn and have fun is to take a field trip to a place connected with one of your subjects. School systems know the value of having students *see, feel, and touch* in the learning process. An experience, which uses all your senses, generates far more interest and knowledge retention than does book learning alone.

So how can you take advantage of the "real world?" It all depends on what you must learn and where your interests lie. Take history, for example, and assume you live in the East. What can you do if you are studying the American Civil War? You can visit one of the many battlefields and learn first hand how the battle was fought, who the important military leaders were, and why the battle was important. *Imagine* what it would be like to be a soldier fighting in that dark period of your history. Civil War battlefields stretch from Pennsylvania to Georgia and from the east coast to Mississippi. You can, of course use the same strategy when studying the Revolutionary War.

Suppose you are studying the history and development of the earth. Visit a museum and learn about the earth's geology. In some museums you can even find replicas of dinosaurs and other creatures that became extinct millions of years ago!

Take advantage of the world all around and you will be rewarded with experiences you will never forget. One student visited England and toured several castles dating back hundreds of years. He remarked at the time, "Why didn't I pay attention in history class?"

Summary

The best time to study is when you are relaxed. Learning comes more naturally and with less effort when you are stress free. Use a schedule to develop a *systematic* plan to study regularly and to finish each assignment, whether it is a term paper or studying for a test. Each assignment will seem easier when you have a plan to complete it.

Find a place where you can study regularly without distractions or interruptions. You must focus and concentrate on material to *learn* it when you *first* study it. Distractions and interruptions will force you to read the material again.

Develop an interest in your subjects. It is much easier to learn when you have an interest. Study in short bursts. A study session is more effective when you divide it into several periods of about thirty minutes each, instead of a one or two hour session.

Plan each study session. Before you begin, know what you expect to accomplish from the session. Use all your time productively whether you are at the dentist or getting your car repaired: it could be a perfect opportunity for a short burst study session.

Avoid interference, that is, studying two similar subjects back-to-back. You could easily confuse chemistry and biology studies or your French and Spanish studies. Study a different subject between the two. Consider joining or forming a study group. Your understanding of almost any subject will increase through discussion and exchange of ideas among students.

Finally, take advantage of the real world. Take a field trip on your own. An experience, which uses all your senses, generates far more interest and knowledge retention than does book learning alone.

You have power you never dreamed of. You can do things you never thought you could do. There are no limitations in what you can do except the limitation in your own mind as to what you cannot do. Don't think you cannot. Think you can.

Darwin P. Kingsley

Chapter Ten

STUDY SKILLS:

THE TECHNIQUES TO EXCEL

What types of skills are necessary? How does one acquire these skills? Why are they important?

Reading And Vocabulary

Probably the most important study skills you can acquire are reading and vocabulary. These skills are the building blocks of achievement. As you progress from elementary school to junior high or middle school, to high school and finally to college or the business world, you will be challenged by the amount of written information you must digest. To meet this challenge, you must be prepared. You must be able to read and comprehend large amounts of information to fulfill your responsibilities within the time available.

You will be faced with various types of reading, and you must use different sets of skills to adapt to each. For example, you will read a technical paper or a textbook more slowly than fiction, which usually does not require the same detailed level of reading. In fact, if you are reading fiction for pleasure, you may find yourself reading very rapidly, almost to the point of skimming to get to the climax. Obviously, such a technique will not work effectively for textbook material, which must be read closely.

You probably know if your reading skills are adequate. If you doubt their adequacy, seek help from special reading programs, your school counselors, or adult education courses. The time you spend in such instruction will be invaluable. To improve you reading skills on your own, set aside a period of twenty to thirty minutes a day for reading. You can read a newspaper, magazine, or a book for pleasure. The more you read, the more quickly you will develop and enhance your reading skills.

As important as it is to read skillfully, it is just as important to know what you are reading. You cannot fully comprehend a work if you do not understand the meanings of the words you are reading. Therefore, a good vocabulary is also a prerequisite for achievement.

So how does one develop such a vocabulary? It is a simple process that builds on itself. Too often, people read a book, magazine, or a newspaper and make no attempt to look up words they do not know. When you read with a dictionary nearby (even a small pocket dictionary), you can immediately find the definition for unfamiliar words. To increase your retention, make it a practice to write down the definitions of the words you look up. Write the definitions on 3x5 cards. You can then review the words and meanings from time to time until you feel confident you know them. Another way to increase your retention of these words is to use them in your writings and conversations.

By increasing your understanding of just one word, you will learn the meanings of other words as you look up the one. This is the quickest and most effective way to build an effective vocabulary. Another way is to get books on vocabulary from your bookstore or library. These books will introduce you to many new words and their proper uses in a relatively short time.

There is still another reason for increasing your vocabulary. It concerns your ability to communicate with other people. How often have you found it difficult to communicate your thoughts or feelings effectively? An effective vocabulary can make this seemingly impossible task possible.

Studies have shown that the people with the best vocabularies reach the highest levels of achievement. People in business go farther up the corporate or management ladder, and students with the best vocabularies get the best grades.

To conclude this discussion of the importance of reading and vocabulary, consider the U. S. Department of Education's findings in their 1987 study, *What Works*.

Six percent of 9-year-olds in 1984 could not follow brief written directions or select phrases to describe pictures. Failure to perform these rudimentary reading exercises places them in danger of future school failure.

Forty percent of 13-year-olds and 16 percent of 17-year-olds attending high school have not acquired intermediate reading skills. They are unable to search for specific information, interrelate ideas, or make generalizations about literature, science, and social studies materials. Inability to perform these tasks raises the question of how well these students can read the range of academic material they are likely to encounter in school.

Just 5 percent of students at age 17 have advanced reading skills and strategies that enable them to synthesize and restructure ideas presented in specialized or complicated tests used by professional and technical workers.

Survey and assess your reading skills. If you need help get it now! Begin your journey toward more effective reading and vocabulary skills today!

Introduction to Note-taking

Note-taking, like other study skills, is an art. The ability to take good notes allows you to focus on important information and not waste time studying and reviewing what is not important.

There are primarily two distinct types of note-taking: note-taking in the classroom or from formal lectures, and note-taking from written materials such as textbooks, journals, magazine articles, or other assigned readings. To take effective notes, you must decide what type of notebook to use and how to record your notes quickly, while capturing the important ideas.

Notebooks

There are different types of notebooks. Whatever type you choose, your *first* order of business is to write your name, address, and telephone number inside the front cover. Should you lose the book, you want to ensure that the finder can contact you. You might even state you will pay a reward to anyone who finds it. The few moments you spend putting your name in your notebooks (and textbooks) will be time well spent. Imagine the horror (yes, horror) of losing your notebook halfway through the semester, or worse yet, just before final exams.

Spiral or Loose-leaf

The two most popular types of notebooks are spiral and loose-leaf. The spiral notebook has one major advantage over the loose-leaf notebook. The pages will not fall out unless you consciously tear one out. While this seems like a definite advantage, consider the benefits of using a loose-leaf notebook and then decide which one you prefer.

With a loose-leaf notebook, you are free to rearrange or reorder your pages as you wish. You can annotate your notes on a subject any time, simply by adding another sheet of paper. You can place handouts directly before or after your lecture or textbook notes on the appropriate topic. You probably know what a disaster can result when you do not keep handouts in order and where you can find them.

Lecture/Classroom Note-taking

This type of note-taking requires a particular skill. You generally have only one opportunity to listen, discern the important issues, and record the information in your notebook. If you miss a point because you were not paying attention, it may be lost forever. It is something like the challenge that awaits every wedding photographer. When the bride comes down the aisle, the photographer has one opportunity to record the event as it happens. If the photographer or his equipment do not respond properly, that precise event can never be recorded as it occurred.

There are two important aspects to developing this skill. You must be able to listen effectively and take notes.

Listening and Observing

You must be alert and attentive! Take a seat as close to the teacher or speaker as possible. Sit up and maintain eye contact with the speaker. This will help you to focus and concentrate on what the speaker is saying and avoid distractions. It is easy to be distracted by a speaker's mannerisms, clothing, or style of speaking.

Learn to adjust to less than perfect listening conditions. You must tune out distractions, such as noise or commotion outside the classroom. As the speaker begins, listen to what is said. Students often *hear* but do not *listen* to the speaker.

Listening is focused hearing. It necessarily implies that you hear the information and actively evaluate it. You must *evaluate* the information to determine what the speaker believes are the important parts of the presentation. Once you decide what is important, you can structure your studies to concentrate on those points. They are sure to be included on an examination.

What else can you do to become an astute listener? Be prepared for the class or lecture. Know something about the topic to be presented. As the speaker delivers the lesson, you will be able to relate the information to your preparation for the class. You should then have a better understanding and appreciation for the speaker's point of view.

Turn the speaker's words into mental pictures, if possible. This visualization process creates powerful memory traces. Visualizing also helps maintain interest in the subject. Instead of passively listening to a lecture on the Boston Tea Party, imagine yourself being there. You could be an observer on the pier or even a colonist dressed like an Indian, who is throwing the tea into the harbor! Try to feel the emotion and excitement of the situation. Your people are protesting unfair taxation. How do you feel?

Now, you might wonder how you can spend time imagining yourself at the Boston Tea Party as you listen to the speaker. The average person speaks at one hundred twenty-five words per minute, while the human brain can think at five hundred words per minute. This is four times as fast! Therefore, you *can* visualize and keep up with the lecture.

IMAGINE YOURSELF AT THE BOSTON TEA PARTY

As you listen, notice when the speaker's voice begins to change pitch or when the speaker seems to become animated or excited. These are clues that the speaker is about to present a point he or she considers important. Be alert to any time when the speaker repeats or emphasizes a point. Usually, a speaker will direct you to an important issue or idea by beginning with phrases such as, "Most importantly . . ., The principle issue is . . ., Remember that . . ., The important readings are . . .."

Recording Your Notes

When taking notes, imagine you are a newspaper reporter. Your objective is to record the speaker's main ideas accurately and concisely.

Sometimes it will be difficult to determine a speaker's main idea or how subordinate ideas relate to it. Do your best to determine the main ideas. Later, you can review your notes and restructure them if necessary.

It will be easier to determine the main idea when you complete your assignments before class. Then, you will have a basis for understanding the ideas presented.

There is an effective note-taking system you should consider using. Walter Pauk developed what he calls *The Cornell Note-taking System*. The system involves dividing a blank notebook page into several sections and then recording different type of notes in each section. It works like this.

Take an eight and one-half by eleven sheet of paper and draw a vertical line about two and one-half inches from the left edge or red margin. Draw a horizontal line about two inches from the bottom of the paper (see Exhibit 10.1). In the top right corner, write the date and the subject. On the right side of the page, record your notes. Record your notes in outline form using brief phrases. After class, go over your notes and fill in missing information.

During the first opportunity to study your notes, write a keyword in the left column, next to a section of notes. This keyword should be adequate to prompt your recall of the details recorded on the right. At the bottom, write a brief summary of the page. When you review the notes from time to time, look at the keywords and try to recall the details recorded in the notes. Study Exhibit 10.1 to understand the mechanics and value of this system.

Using Shorthand

To take notes quickly, without missing the main ideas, you should develop your own system of shorthand to abbreviate words and phrases. Your system will allow you to take notes quickly, without the need for spelling out each word. Some examples for converting words into a form of shorthand are shown on page 159.

	11/1 US HIST
	Causes of the Civil War
Sectional	1. Ecomonic Differences 2. Ways of Life
Slavery/ States Rights	1. Compromise of 1850 2. Kansas-Nebraska Act 3. Dred Scott Decision

Sectional division of the North and South, and disputes over slavery and states rights led to the Civil War.

Exhibit 10.1

inc	increase	mtl	material, metal
dec	decrease	c/s	common stock
w/	with	p/s	preferred stock
w/i	within	pr	price
w/o	without	pmt	payment
o/s	outstanding	argmt	agreement,
info	information		argument
>	greater than	<	less than

Textbook Study and Note-taking

Studying and taking notes from textbooks presents a different type of challenge from the lecture format. While you have to be discriminating in what you record, you have more than one opportunity to correct a mistake.

In 1948, Francis Robinson developed a study system called SQ3R, which stands for Survey, Question, Read, Recite, and Review. This system is extremely effective, and its use will greatly increase your comprehension and retention of textbook material. You will become an active reader, and you will learn to probe the text for important details.

When you first use SQ3R it may take longer to complete a chapter. As you will see, it may take only a *few* extra minutes when you *initially* use the process. As the process becomes a habit, you will discover that your study time will be reduced; you will understand much more the *first time* you read the material.

When you review, it will not be necessary to reread a chapter or wade through it to find the important ideas.

The five stages of SQ3R follow.

Survey

When you are assigned a reading in a *new* textbook, where do you begin? Do you begin at the first page of Chapter 1? When you are assigned to read another chapter in the textbook, do you begin by reading the first page of the chapter and continue to the end?

If the answer to each of these questions is yes, you are missing an important opportunity to (1) determine the author's purpose and viewpoint, and (2) further your ability to understand the information presented.

In Tony Buzan's book, *Using Both Sides of Your Brain*, Buzan likens studying a textbook to putting a puzzle together. When you assemble a puzzle, you look at the picture on the box to see how pieces fit together. Next, you separate the side pieces from the middle pieces and begin putting it together, usually beginning at one corner. In this process, however, you may start at one corner, but you do not work from that one corner only. You may work on several areas of the puzzle at the same time and see how each section relates to each other section.

The purpose of the survey step is to obtain a general understanding of the contents of a book or chapter. You must understand how each part relates to the total. When you determine the purpose and direction of the complete work, the parts are easier to understand. As with a puzzle, you must know how the parts relate to each other.

 Before beginning a *new* textbook, read the preface and introduction. These sections will explain the author's purpose in writing the book, and express any particular viewpoints the author has. Next, read the table of contents to determine the book's organization and contents. Then, skim each chapter taking particular note of the headings and subheadings that appear in boldface. Finally, read the summaries at the end of each chapter. This whole process might take one-half hour, and only has to be done when you *begin* each new book. This small expenditure of time will provide a foundation upon which to build your understanding of the total book.

So, you have surveyed the book and must now begin your study of Chapter 1. Should you begin by plunging directly into reading the chapter? Absolutely not! Begin by surveying the chapter. Skim the material as you did when you were surveying the entire book, but at a slower pace. When the chapter has an introduction describing its contents, read it. Next, read all the titles and headings. Pay attention to the flow and progression of the information. Finally, read the chapter summary. The summary will pull together in a few paragraphs all the important ideas presented in the chapter.

The value of reading the headings is immeasurable. Titles and headings tell you what you are about to read. They serve to guide you through the material and focus your interest. Imagine trying to read a textbook without titles or headings. It would be difficult to find each place where the author is changing topics.

In Kenneth Higbee's book, *Your Memory*, he discusses the value even a short title can have in directing attention and improving comprehension and retention. Read the following paragraph and decide how much easier it would have been to understand and recall the process if a short title was provided.

The process to be followed is really very simple. You must first sort things into different groups. One group may actually be enough, but this depends on the types of items you must sort. If you lack the proper facilities, you will have to go somewhere else to complete the job. It is important not to do too much at one time. Doing so can cause severe complications. After you complete this stage of the process, you may again have to arrange the items into different groups. You can then put each item into its proper storage place, where it can be obtained for future use. As each item is used over again, you will have to repeat the entire process.

Would you have understood the material better if you knew the subject was washing clothes? Read the material again now that you know the subject.

 The value of reading the chapter summary is threefold. First, it allows you to preview the material and provides your introduction to the chapter. Second, it summarizes the main ideas. You will then be on guard to look for them during your actual reading of the chapter. As you have read before, understanding and retention is higher when you can associate new information with information you already know. When you read the chapter, you can associate the information with the ideas you already acquired from reading the chapter summary. Third, your mind functions better when it processes general information (chapter summary) followed by specific information (actual reading). It should take no more than a few minutes to complete the survey stage.

Question

This next stage of SQ3R is designed to make you an active reader. You become an active reader by formulating questions about the material based on the titles and headings contained in each chapter.

Here is how it works. Skim the chapter again and develop questions based on the headings and titles. Suppose you are taking a geography course and the assigned reading is about New

Zealand. Several headings and titles are: Founding, Climate, Terrain, Culture, and Religion. As you skim the titles ask yourself the following questions. *When was New Zealand founded and by whom? What kind of weather does it have? What is its terrain, is it flat, rocky, mountainous? What is its culture, what are its people like? What is the popular religion in this country? Why is it popular? What other religions are there?* Basically, your questions should ask, Who, What, Where, When, Why or How.

When you ask these types of questions, you naturally begin to look for the answers as you read the material. This is the role of an active reader. You search for answers and you expect the chapter to provide them. Formulating your own questions has another benefit. It helps to build your interest level in the material because you expect answers to questions you believe are important.

As an alternative to formulating your own questions, you can use the author's questions found at the end of the chapter. These questions will direct you to the information the author believes is important.

Keep in mind that up to this point, you have only spent a *few* minutes studying the chapter.

Read

Your next task is to begin reading the material. Many students, armed with fluorescent or colored markers, highlight what they believe to be the important parts of a chapter on the first reading. Do not fall into this trap. Read the entire chapter or a complete section, at a minimum, before you begin to underline, highlight, or otherwise mark the important ideas or issues presented.

 Highlighting or underlining on a *first* reading is not effective. Most students have a natural tendency to skip over what they highlight. They rationalize that they have identified a major point and will return to study and learn the information later. This process is counterproductive. Students should learn and understand information the first time they encounter it. When they revisit material, it should not be for rereading. It should be to recall, practice, and rehearse the material to build comprehension and knowledge retention.

Another problem with underlining or highlighting on the first pass is that what may appear to be important, may not be so. As a result, you may highlight too much or too little. You must have a complete grasp of the author's thesis (from reading a complete chapter or section) to understand what is actually important.

USE YOUR HIGHLIGHTERS PRUDENTLY

As you begin to read, pay particular attention to the first and last sentences of each paragraph. These two sentences contain important information. Consider reading them aloud. Speaking and hearing yourself read this information will increase your level of understanding.

The first sentence is commonly called a topic sentence, and it will reveal the main idea or thought of the paragraph. The last sentence will normally bring closure to the discussion. As you read, keep in mind the questions you posed in the question stage. As you search for and find the answers, your understanding and retention of the material will increase. Continue reading the section or chapter until you come to the end.

Now that you have a good understanding of the main idea, go back and read the section or chapter again. This time, highlight or underline the important points as you read. You can use symbols to mark a significant point (e.g., an asterisk) or an area you do not understand (e.g., a question mark).

If you are a public school student, you are not permitted to highlight or markup your textbook. However, you can use a very soft pencil and *lightly* underline or make notations near the text. When you are finished reading, studying, and taking notes from the text, you can use a *MAGIC RUB* eraser, made by FaberCastell, to erase the marks in the book completely.

Recite

This stage of SQ3R involves reciting the material you have learned. You may choose to recite aloud or silently. The purpose of this stage is to initiate your recall of the material. After you have finished marking the text, look at the headings or titles and try to recall the main points. It is important to do this immediately after reading the material because it is fresh in your mind. When you actively recall the material, you begin to formulate the memory traces necessary to retain the material.

After you have successfully recited the material (including highlights and underlines), transfer your notes in the text to 3x5 cards. Use a new card for each new idea. At the top left of the card, record the main idea. At the top right, record the chapter number and the card number within the chapter. For example, a chapter or section entitled "Causes of the Civil War," would be written at the top left of the card. If this was the first note card in Chapter 11, it would be numbered 11.1. The next card would become 11.2 and so on. It is important to keep the cards in numerial order to reflect the sequence of your studies, as well as for ease of reference.

Next, record the necessary information. Record the main idea in as few words as possible to capture the essence of the idea. Do not use complete sentences. Write in outline form so your eyes can see the necessary information at a glance. Exhibit 10.2 is an example of a 3x5 card complete with a mnemonic to prompt recall of the material.

When making more detailed notes on 3x5 cards, use your own words. ***Do not copy verbatim from the book!*** Copying directly from the book merely parrots the words of the author, and you may not really understand what he or she is saying. Taking notes in your own words proves your genuine understanding of the material. If *you* do not understand the material, ask questions because you can be certain there are *others* who do not understand it.

CAUSES OF THE CIVIL WAR   11.1

I. SECTIONAL DIVISION OF NORTH/SOUTH
   A. <u>E</u>conomies   <u>E</u>(agles)
   B. <u>W</u>ay of Life   <u>W</u>(ill)

II. SLAVERY/STATES RIGHTS
   A. <u>C</u>ompromise of 1850   <u>C</u>(arry)
   B. <u>K</u>ansas-Nebraska Act   <u>K</u>(angaroos)
   C. <u>D</u>red Scott Decision   <u>D</u>(aily)

Exhibit 10.2

Using 3x5 cards to record your notes has several distinct advantages. First, as you complete each card after performing your recitation, you are further establishing the information in your memory. Second, each card presents only one piece or snapshot of the information, which is easier to recall when you can see one piece at a time. Third, index cards are easy to review because you do not feel overwhelmed by page after page of traditional notebook type notes. Of course you will have many index cards, but you will find that cards provide for an easier and more effective method of review.

As an alternative to using 3x5 cards, consider using the Cornell System described in the section on "Lecture/Classroom Note-taking." Recall that choosing a particular study strategy or technique is a personal matter. There is no one correct way. You should experiment and decide what works best for you.

Review

Now it is time to review. The essence of this stage is to recall the material frequently by reviewing your 3x5 cards. The more frequently you review, the easier it will be to recall the information. When it comes time for a test, you *will not* be laboring to absorb as much material as you can in a short time. By then, you will have rehearsed the material so often that only a few hours of study will be necessary.

When you review the 3x5 cards, look at the main idea only, then try to recall all the information without looking at the card. Recite the information aloud. If you have difficulty recalling the material, look at the card, and then recite the information again without looking at the card. Repeat this process until you feel comfortable you know the material.

When you recite aloud, several things happen. First, you force yourself to *focus* on the material. Second, you use other senses, speaking and hearing to increase your understanding. If you doubt the effectiveness of reciting your notes aloud, consider the following.

Have you ever read something and did not understand the essence of the material? It could have been a set of directions or a newspaper or magazine article. You then took the reading to a family member or friend and said, "Listen to this and see if you can make any sense of it." As you read the piece to your friend, the meaning suddenly became clear to you. When you did this, speaking and hearing helped you better understand the material.

The review/recall process is more effective than simply reading the cards again and again. Actively recalling and reciting information enables you to remember specific information *when* you need to remember it.

Mind Maps

Another type of note-taking is called mind mapping. Because mind mapping is so versatile, it can be used to record lecture notes, textbook notes, as well as to develop outlines for speeches, essays, and term papers.

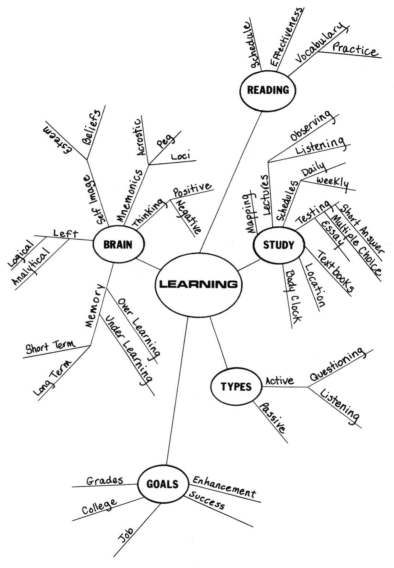

Exhibit 10.3

Mind maps were developed by Tony Buzan, an internationally known expert in the area of learning and the potential of the mind. In his book, *Using Both Sides of Your Brain*, Buzan illustrates and describes the benefits of mind mapping.

The idea behind mind mapping is to draw a picture or graphical representation of the information to be recorded. Exhibit 10.3 illustrates a mind map for an initial draft of this book.

The objective of a mind map is to use keywords to record a main idea, and then connect subordinate ideas to the main idea with other key words. As you review Exhibit 10.3, notice how the main idea for the book is *learning* and how all the secondary ideas are connected to it. Each secondary idea, in turn, has subordinate ideas linked to it.

The map allows you to interrelate all the secondary ideas with the main idea. In other words, you can *see* how ideas are connected to each other. In this respect, mapping has a distinct advantage over the more traditional form of note-taking in outline form. With an outline, you record each idea in list form and tend to concentrate on one idea or topic at a time. With the map, you see and consider all ideas simultaneously and record new ones as you think of them. When finished, you can use the map to put your topics in traditional outline form.

As you prepare the map, highlight sections of the map with different colors. The colors will help you to *see* the different sections, and perhaps even rank them in their order of importance.

Another advantage of the mind map is that new information can be added easily by connecting another line to the appropriate idea. With the traditional outline, you must go back and try to squeeze in new information.

Other Uses For Mind Maps

Mind maps are so versatile they can be used to prepare speeches, lectures, essays, book reports, term papers or almost any other project.

Just for fun, suppose you must prepare an essay on the subject of a professional sport. First, try putting together an outline of the essay by using the traditional approach. Spend about five minutes listing what you believe are all the important facets of the sport. When you are finished, pick another sport for a speech or essay. This time, prepare a mind map of the subject. Isn't it much easier to tap your mental reservoir using a mind map?

Summary

One of the most important study skills you can acquire is reading. *Reading* is a building block of achievement. Survey and assess your reading skills. If you need help, get it now!

Vocabulary is another building block of achievement. While it is important to read skillfully, it is just as important to know what you are reading. You must understand the meanings of many words. Studies have shown that a good vocabulary is a prerequisite for academic or business achievement.

The ability to take good notes is an art. It allows you to focus on important information and not waste time studying and reviewing unimportant information.

Taking notes requires using a notebook, and several types are available. Consider using a loose leaf instead of a spiral or bound notebook. Choose the one you believe best suits your needs and *use it*!

When taking notes, use your own form of shorthand and consider using *The Cornell Note-taking System*. Whatever method you choose, make sure your notes are organized and copy them over if you have difficulty reading them. Lecture note-taking requires a particular skill because you generally have only one opportunity to listen, discern the important issues, and record the information.

Studying and taking notes from textbooks presents a different type of challenge. While you have to be discriminating in what you record, you have more than one opportunity to correct a mistake. Try using the Survey, Question, Read, Recite and Review (SQ3R) method of study and note-taking for textbooks. Keep your notes on 3x5 cards.

Mind maps are particularly effective for visually diagraming the important aspects of an assignment. These maps allow you to think about an entire set of ideas at the same time. You can then interrelate ideas with each other, instead of thinking about them one at time. Try mind mapping. It is fun and effective.

If you've got a job to do,
Do it now!
If it's one you wish were through,
Do it now!
If you're sure the job's your own,
Do not hem and haw and groan-
Do it now!
Don't put off a bit of work,
Do it now!
It doesn't pay to shirk,
Do it now!
If you want to fill a place
And be useful to the race,
Just get up and take a brace-
Do it now!
Don't linger by the way,
Do it now!
You'll lose if you delay,
Do it now!
If the other fellows wait,
Or postpone until it's late,
You hit up a faster gait-
Do it now!

Unknown

Chapter Eleven

TEST-TAKING: THE FINAL CHALLENGE

What are test-taking strategies and skills? Can knowing *how* to take an exam really increase test scores? How can anything other than pure knowledge help to get better grades?

An Introduction To Testing

Testing is where you finally get to show your mastery of the learning process. It is fitting that the last major chapter concerns testing: the usual culmination of a learning process or course is a test.

There are general strategies and skills you can use on any exam to ensure you receive the maximum number of points available. There are also specific strategies to use for essay, multiple choice, short answer exam, true-false or matching exams.

GENERAL STRATEGIES

The following general strategies will help you to receive the maximum number of points. Please do not dismiss these strategies as insignificant: they can increase your performance level which can result in higher grades.

Get Enough Rest

The night before the exam, plan to get a good night's sleep. You will perform best when you are rested.

Eat and Drink Sensibly

On the morning of the exam (assuming a morning examination) eat a nourishing but light breakfast. The rule is to eat and drink sensibly. *Do not* drink too much coffee, as this will increase your trips to the rest room (if allowed) and disrupt your concentration. If you are not allowed a rest room break, your discomfort is likely to affect your performance.

If you have an afternoon exam, eat a light lunch. You know how sleepy you become just after eating. Instead of having to digest your lunch, your blood will be available for your brain to digest test questions!

Prepare A Checklist

Prepare a checklist of the items you must have at the exam, be it in another classroom in your school or at another site. A teacher may have instructed you to bring certain materials for the exam, a calculator, for example. For standardized exams, you might have to have an admission slip, pencils and picture identification card. Review your checklist before you leave home to ensure you have everything.

One fellow drove forty miles to an exam site. Although he arrived about one hour before exam time, he was horrified to discover he left his admission slip at home. He drove home and returned about one-half hour after the exam had begun. At that point, he was neither physically nor mentally prepared to take the exam. He did not do well.

Arrive Early

Plan to arrive early for the exam. If you have to go to an unfamiliar place, make sure you know how to get there. You do not need the added stress of getting lost and being late.

Psyche Yourself Up

Just before the exam, get into a positive frame of mind. Do not use the time to start worrying about what might be on the exam. Instead, think about what makes you really feel good. Think about your favorite song, your favorite things to do, the special people in your life. A positive, upbeat frame of mind will help you to do your best.

These suggestions may seem silly or foolish. Be assured they are not. Suppose you have to give a speech to a hundred people or more. You are prepared but anxious. Just before the speech, you listen to your favorite music. You feel good every time you hear it. How will listening to the music affect your performance? You will feel great and the audience will perceive your enthusiasm immediately!

Now suppose that instead of listening to your favorite music, you watch a depressing movie. What effect would this movie have on your state of mind and performance immediately afterward? If you are unhappy or depressed before you begin, it becomes more difficult to do your best. Just before the exam, consciously choose a positive, upbeat frame of mind.

Avoid Others

Avoid listening to the idle chatter of students quizzing each other outside the exam room. Avoid those who attempt to disguise their own shortcomings by trying to make you feel as if you are not prepared.

Sit Close to the Front

If you can choose your seat, sit as close to the front of the room as possible. From this seat, you will hear all instructions. If you believe there will be distractions, ask if you can move to another seat.

Remain Relaxed

If you feel anxious or nervous, take a few deep breaths. Breathe in slowly through your nose, hold it for a few seconds, and then exhale through your mouth. Do this several times. Deep breathing has a soothing and calming effect. If you can, take the opportunity to stretch your muscles several times during the exam. Shift your position in your seat. Close your eyes and relax your body and mind for a few minutes. You might be surprised to discover how a few minutes of rest can recharge your mental abilities.

Listen To All Instructions And Read All Directions

Have you ever been on an airplane flight? Have you ever noticed what happens when the flight attendants begin to give safety instructions to the passengers? The next time you are on a flight, look around. You will see few people paying attention.

The attendants describe how to use the seat belts, the emergency oxygen mask and flotation devices. They point out the location of emergency exits and recommend that the passengers read the information card placed near their seats. The card further describes what to do in an emergency and the specific location of exits. How many people have you seen listening to the attendants or reading this information? Perhaps, you have seen only a few.

So, what are the consequences of failing to listen to the flight attendants or reading the information card? Those who fail to listen or read are courting disaster! People who know what to do ahead of time will fare the best in an emergency.

This analogy is equally applicable to a testing situation. Those individuals that do not listen to oral instructions or read the specific directions are also courting disaster. You must know what is expected and how to respond, if you are to receive proper credit for the information you present on an examination.

Listen carefully to oral instructions from your teacher or examiner. Carefully and slowly read the directions contained on the test itself. Determine how you are to answer questions. If the test is multiple choice, determine if you are to circle, check, or fill a symbol to answer a question. Failure to mark the answer appropriately may cost many points.

On some exams you are told there is only one correct answer. When you are given this information, do not spend time looking for more than one.

When you are instructed to number your pages a certain way, make sure you do so. Again, failure to follow directions can cost points. Many studies have shown that an outstanding deficiency of low test scorers is their failure to pay adequate attention to directions!

Survey The Exam

When you are permitted to open the exam, do not plunge right ahead and begin answering questions. Take a few minutes to *survey* (look over) the entire exam. There are several reasons for doing this.

First, the survey can help boost your confidence by seeing how much you do know. If you are still feeling anxious or nervous, you can begin the exam by answering the easiest questions first. This will certainly boost your confidence. There is no rule that states you must begin an exam with question number one.

Second, by surveying the entire exam you may find the answers to some questions in other questions! Finally, surveying the exam will help you to decide how much time to spend on each section.

Allocate Your Time

You must allocate your time properly. Whether you are taking an exam for your regular classwork or a specialized exam such as the SAT, ACT, LSAT, or other exam, it is vital that you gauge your time for each section. To obtain maximum credit, you must finish the entire exam.

At the beginning of the exam determine how much time is available. Then, decide how much time you will allow yourself to complete each question or section. Remember to allow yourself ample time to review your answers at the end of the exam. The amount of review  time will vary from exam to exam. There will be times when an exam will contain essay and multiple choice questions. In this situation, allow enough time to read over your essays and double-check your multiple choice answers.

Periodically monitor your progress by checking your watch. If you are falling behind, try to spend less time on each question. Do not become a slave to your watch! Use it as tool to gauge your progress so you can adjust your timing as necessary.

Read The Questions!

Of course you will read the question! How else could you get an answer? But, did you really *read* the question?

Make sure you *completely understand* each question. Underline or highlight all keywords. You can easily fool yourself into choosing the wrong answer. For example, consider the following multiple choice question.

Which of the following individuals was not a President of the United States?

a.   Thomas Jefferson
b.   John Garfield
c.   Alexander Hamilton
d.   Rutherford B. Hayes

Obviously the most famous name on the list is Thomas Jefferson. It would be very easy to read the question and skip over the *not*. Then, seeing Jefferson, pick that answer without further thought. The correct answer of course is *c*. Alexander Hamilton was the first Secretary of the Treasury, and Garfield and Hayes were Presidents, although not as famous as Jefferson.

When you see a question like this, underline the keywords *not*, *President*, and *United States*. Underlining these words will keep you focused on the important parts of the question.

Consider a more extreme example. Suppose an exam poses an essay question such as, *List three reasons why the United States did not want to enter World War II*. This question probably could be worth anywhere from ten percent to fifty percent of an exam grade. If you read the question quickly and decide you are being asked why the United States entered World War II, you will be fortunate to receive any credit for your answer. You will have answered the opposite question! Again underline or highlight the keywords as you read the question. The keywords here are *three reasons, United States, not,* and *World War II*. Of course, make sure you list *three* reasons!

Work At Your Own Pace

Work at your own pace and do not be concerned or distracted by those who finish the exam before you. They may have done well or could just have easily rushed through the exam and have done poorly. Remember, nobody gets a medal or extra points for finishing the exam first.

Maintain Faith And Confidence

 Have faith and confidence in yourself. Recall your past exam successes. You are prepared and you are ready. No matter how hard the exam appears to be, *do not give up!* The worst thing you can do is quit because you think you do not know the answers. Throughout the exam continue to put forth your best effort. If the exam is difficult for you, it will be difficult for others. Since most teachers grade exams on a curve, your efforts will produce satisfactory results.

Keep Your Paper Neat

No matter what type of exam you must take, ensure all your test papers are neat and have a pleasing appearance. A teacher will be favorably impressed with a paper he or she can read easily.

A good rule to follow is to put yourself in the shoes of the examiner. Imagine it is late in the evening. You have already graded thirty or forty other exams. You are tired. You have one more paper to grade. Are you more likely to accept legible and neat answers or those with numerous arrows and insertions to direct you all over the page? Sloppy work may not enable the examiner to follow your thought process or determine your actual answer!

Answer All Questions

Answer every question on the exam. You cannot receive credit for a blank. However, if you put down something, you might receive partial credit. This is especially true for essay type questions.

Refer to the discussion on multiple choice examinations to learn about the penalty for guessing on those types of exams.

Draw Diagrams

When you have difficulty understanding a question, or following a process described in a question, try drawing a diagram of the problem. Use arrows and other symbols to refer to people or things being described. Using a diagram enables you to solve a problem visually, which is a powerful tool.

Consider the following business law question. The subject is agency, a situation where one person has the authority to act for another.

Smith signed a contract with Jones on behalf of Mitchell. In doing so, Smith acted outside the scope of his authority. Mitchell may be held responsible on the contract if:

a.   Mitchell retains the benefits of the contract.

b.   Mitchell ratifies the entire contract after Jones withdraws from the contract.

c.   Jones elects to hold Mitchell liable on the contract.

d.   Jones was aware of the limitation on Smith's authority.

Before you can begin to consider the correct answer, it is important to understand the relationships of the individuals involved, i. e., who is acting for whom. To avoid confusion, diagram the relationship.

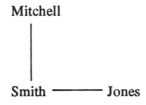

You can *see* the relationships between the three individuals. It is clear that Smith is acting for Mitchell when he contracts with Jones. You can now begin to consider the choices in *a through d*. The correct business law answer is *a*.

Visualize Your Notes

When mentally searching for an answer, try to visualize your notes or 3x5 cards. This will help you to form a mental picture of the material and help you to recall.

Use The "Context" Of Learning In Recall

Besides visualizing your notes, you can vividly imagine the conditions under which you learned the material. These conditions are called the *context* of learning. Were you in your room, your office, or the library? Was it warm or cool? What did the room smell like? These recollections will improve your ability to recall the information you need. Have you experienced the sensation that comes with smelling an aroma or scent to which you have not been exposed for a long time? You may have been walking down the street and became aware of someone's perfume or cologne. Suddenly the smell evoked a strong memory of someone you have not seen for a while, a former girlfriend or boyfriend, or a relative perhaps.

A psychologist at Yale University conducted an experiment to determine whether smells could serve as memory retrieval clues. Several groups of students memorized a list of words. Some did so in a room with the smell of chocolate in the air; others did so with no particular scent present. The psychologist found that students exposed to the chocolate smell in both the learning and testing situation scored *fifty percent* higher than those who had no scent in either session! Recalling the conditions under which you learn material can improve your ability to recall that material.

Check Your Answers For Common Sense

Too often, students rush to complete a question and put down an answer without really giving thought to its reasonableness. Consider the following:

Fifth graders had studied various American Indian tribes. On an exam, they were given a map of the United States with the locations of the Indian tribes shown. The Eastern Woodland Indians were shown as living on the east coast. An exam question asked:

In what part of the United States do the Eastern Woodland Indians live?

a.   Central United States
b.   Southern United States
c.   Western United States
d.   Eastern United States

Amazing as it may seem, some students responded with answer *c*. This answer is of course silly, because where would the *Eastern* Woodland Indians live? They would live in the East, of course. Answer *d* is the only response that made sense.

While this example may seem simplistic, many choices provided on multiple choice exams are out of the reasonable range, and yet students select such choices. On other types of exams, particularly math exams, ask yourself the question, *Does this answer make sense?*

Forget The Exam

After you finish the exam and leave the examination room, do not torture yourself by second guessing your answers or by letting others second guess your answers. The test is over. Forget it until you receive your grade.

Learn From Your Exams

After you receive your grade, look over your wrong answers and decide why the answers are not correct. You must know why an answer is incorrect if you are to learn from the testing experience. *Learn from your previous exams!*

By studying your old exams you can gain an insight into how your teacher operates and what types of questions he or she may include from lectures or textbooks. Knowing your teacher's or examiner's style is every bit as important as knowing the information itself!

MULTIPLE CHOICE EXAMS

Multiple choice exams require you to use a different set of memory or analytical skills than do essay or short answer exams. Multiple choice exams require you to use recognition instead of recall skills. That is, while you do not have to remember the answer, you must be able to recognize it. Do not be fooled, however! A good multiple choice exam is designed to include answers called *distractors*. These answers are intended to test your ability to discern the *correct* answer from a *possible* answer. In other words, the correct answer will not stand out or be the obvious choice. Read the following question, which is similar to a multiple choice question the authors had on a driver's license exam.

As you approach an intersection with a green light, a pedestrian is crossing the street in a crosswalk. You should:

a.   Scold him for jaywalking.
b.   Run him down, as he is crossing against the light.
c.   Grant him the right of way.
d.   Proceed through the intersection and avoid hitting him.

It is obvious b is not the correct answer or even a possibility. But what about a, c, and d? Jaywalking *is* illegal *(a)*. Granting the right of way would ensure his safety *(c)*. Finally, proceeding through the intersection without hitting him does not seem unreasonable *(d)*. The correct answer is *c*, but answers *a* and *d* are intended to distract you and determine if you really do know the answer.

Whole books have been written on how to deal with the multiple choice format exam. The following are basic rules and skills to employ when taking a multiple choice exam.

Do Not Look At The Answers

Read the question, underline or highlight the keywords, and make sure you understand it. If possible, try to answer the question *without looking at the answers*. If you can do this, it may prevent you from becoming confused when you see the all the possible answers. Knowing the answer is not enough! You must be able to discern the incorrect answers from the correct one.

Multiple Choice Answers Are Really True/False Questions

Evaluate *each* answer as you would a true/false question. As you read each answer, ask yourself, *Is this answer true?* If you think it is, leave it for consideration. If you think the answer is false, immediately eliminate it from consideration. Consider the previous sample question about the presidents to illustrate this technique.

Which of the following individuals was not a President of the United States?

a.   Thomas Jefferson

b.   John Garfield

c.   Alexander Hamilton

d.   Rutherford B. Hayes

Remember, you must evaluate each answer as true/false. You are to choose which person was not a United States President. You have highlighted *not*, *President*, and *United States*.

Answer *a* is false. Jefferson was a president. Eliminate this answer. Answer *b* is false, as Garfield was a president. Eliminate this answer also. Answer *c* is true. Hamilton was *not* a president. This answer remains for consideration until you evaluate the final answer. Answer *d* is false because Hayes was a president. Eliminate this answer. Since *c* is the only "true" answer, it is the correct response.

This true/false strategy is especially helpful when your response can include one or more of the choices. Using our previous question, examine a new set of possible answers.

Which of the following individuals was not a President of the United States?

I.   Thomas Jefferson
II.   John Garfield
III.   Alexander Hamilton
IV.   Rutherford B. Hayes

a.   III and IV
b.   I and III
c.   III only
d.   II and IV

Consider whether answers *a* through *d* are true or false. Eliminate the false answers. By using the true/false strategy to eliminate answers, you can dramatically increase the odds of answering the question correctly. For example, when you have four choices and no  idea which answer is correct, you have a one in four or twenty-five percent chance of picking the correct answer. When you eliminate one answer, your chances rise to thirty-three percent, and when you can eliminate two of the four answers, your chances rise dramatically to fifty percent! Therefore, instead of taking a wild guess, try to eliminate answers and guess intelligently.

Look for Conditional and Absolute Words

A conditional word is one that qualifies an answer. For example, a question may ask, *Which of the following is the best explanation of* . . .. *Best* is the conditional word. This question puts you on notice that more than one answer may be correct. However, only one will be the *best*. In most exams, the word *best* will not be specifically set out for you in italics or underlined. You must highlight or underline the word to draw your attention to it. Therefore, be careful not to read the question and then rush to choose the first answer that *appears* correct. Remember, the question does not ask you to choose a correct answer, but the *best* answer.

Look for words such as *all* and *always*. They are *absolutes*. They mean exactly what they say. If something in the question suggests that *all* or *always* is not appropriate, the answer is not correct.

To gain a fuller insight into the psychology and skills of answering multiple choice questions, read *Muscling the Multiple Choice*, by John Garland.

Know the Penalty for Guessing

On some exams, the SAT in particular, you are advised there is a penalty for guessing. That is, incorrect responses will be deducted from your score. You must be aware of the potential penalty for guessing.

In *Muscling the Multiple Choice*, John Garland explains that this penalty is not clearly understood. He advises that on the SAT, for example, the penalty is not a point for point reduction in score for each incorrect answer. Instead, the penalty consists of a portion of the total possible credit for a question. When a question has four possible answers, an incorrect response will result in a reduction of one-fourth of a point, not one whole point. When a question has five possible responses, the penalty then becomes one-fifth of a point. Therefore, Garland concludes that when students can reduce or eliminate the number of possible answers, the student can dramatically increase his or her odds of answering the question correctly. In effect, the benefits from making an *intelligent* guess may outweigh the possible consequences of a small penalty for guessing incorrectly.

Under any circumstance, *guessing should only be used as a final resort!* Guessing is not a substitute for adequate preparation. When used wisely, however, it *may* increase some test scores.

Record Your Answers Carefully

If you are provided a computerized answer sheet, make sure you properly enter all identifying information and note the ordering of the answers. *Determine if the answers are numbered across in rows or down in columns.* You will not be allowed extra time at the end of an exam to erase and reorder your answers. Imagine how frantic you would become if you suddenly realize you have misnumbered your answers!

 If you skip a question, make sure you skip that same answer on the answer sheet. A good way to ensure you record your answers properly is to first mark the correct answer in the book. Then, mark the corresponding answer on the answer sheet, making sure the question number and the answer number are the same. After you complete the test, check each answer marked in the book with the answer marked on the answer sheet. You may be surprised to learn you marked the answer correctly in the question book, but marked a different answer on the answer sheet! You do not want to lose credit because you *marked* an incorrect answer.

Do Not Change Your Answers

When you review each answer at the end of the exam, do not change one unless you are absolutely sure the original response was incorrect. Studies have shown that when in doubt, a person's first answer is more likely to be the correct response.

ESSAY EXAMS

Most students dread the thought of taking an essay exam or answering essay questions. They would usually prefer an objective exam (multiple choice or true/false) instead. Since students understand that objective exams require recognition instead of recall of the correct answer, they somehow believe objective exams are easier.

Objective exams are not easier: an answer is either right or wrong. There is no in-between. There is no room for judgement by the grader or teacher as to a correct answer.

Essay exams offer you a unique opportunity. Sometimes you are required to show what you know and the depth of your understanding. At other times, you are asked to argue for or against a particular issue and are graded based on the points you raise in your argument.

Within certain limitations, there are no clearly defined correct or incorrect answers. Teachers/graders can choose to award or not award points based on factual information and *their opinion* whether you have adequately answered a question.

Essay exams provide you an excellent opportunity to shine. Do not fear them. When you prepare an essay that states your main points, constructs a logical discussion of the issues, and draws a conclusion that flows from your explanation, you will be successful.

The following discussion presents specific skills you can use to develop legible, well written, and convincing essay responses.

Answer All Questions

Remember this rule: if you absolutely do not know the answer to an essay question, redefine the question so you can answer it and show that you did study the material. Any answer will probably receive some credit, while failing to answer will result in no credit.

This situation can occur even if you believe you are prepared for an exam. Suppose you were assigned to read *Tom Sawyer* by Mark Twain. On the exam, the teacher or examiner asks you to discuss the development of Tom's character in the book. Even if you are not sure what *development of Tom's character* means, prove you have read the book by discussing the things Tom did. If you do not answer the question, the instructor may assume you did not bother to read the book. When you can show that you did the assignment, you are likely to receive substantial credit for your answer.

Plan And Outline Your Answer

Even when the essay question is on a topic with which you are thoroughly familiar, *do not* plunge head first and immediately begin writing. You must *plan* the best way to present your answer. Unless you are a truly exceptional writer, your work will be littered with erasures, crossouts, and insertion marks.

Begin by reading the question and deciding what the main points of the essay will be. Next, in the margin next to the question or on a scrap piece of paper, jot down the key issues or ideas you will use to present your discussion. Give some thought to using a mind map to list all the related ideas. Next, arrange the issues or ideas in the order you plan to discuss them. Finally, decide what your conclusion (if necessary) will be.

Every essay should contain at least two distinct sections, the introduction and the body or discussion. Additionally, a summary or a conclusion may be needed.

The introduction can simply be a restatement of the issue or how you intend to discuss it. The body contains your discussion of the issues. Separate major issues or ideas by beginning a new paragraph. Finally, when you are asked for an opinion or to take a position on an issue, present a conclusion. The conclusion tells the grader how you believe each issue relates to your main idea. Note that a conclusion is more than a summary.

In a long essay you might want to include a summary to refresh the grader's memory of the main points just before presenting your conclusion.

Your essay should be concise and to the point. Keep your sentences to as few words as possible. Graders do not appreciate having to interpret what you might mean. Instead, they appreciate answers that speak for themselves.

Review the following sample essay question and response to develop your own style for answering such questions.

SAMPLE QUESTION[2]

QUESTION:
Discuss the causes for World War I.

SUGGESTED KEYWORD/PHRASE OUTLINE:
Four causes.

1. Nationalism
    a. loyalty to country
    b. loyalty to political and economic goals
    c. form of patriotism
    d. Balkan Peninsula, Powder Keg of Europe
    e. independence from Ottoman Empire
    f. boundary disputes

2. Military buildup
    a. nationalism encouraged buildup
    b. German buildup
    c. countries follow German lead
    d. technological advances

3. Competition for colonies
  a. race for colonies in Asia and Africa
  b. competition strained relations

4. Military alliances
  a. sense of security
  b. force a country to go to war
  c. Triple Alliance

*Note: Your handwritten outline may not look as pretty or be as complete as this one. However, the outline will definitely help you to **plan and organize** your answer.*

SUGGESTED ANSWER:

[Introduction]

The four basic causes for the outbreak of World War I were: nationalism, military build-ups, competition for colonies in Asia and Africa, and military alliances between the countries.

[Body]

Nationalism was a strong sense of loyalty to a country's political and economic goals. This was an extreme sense of patriotism that caused conflicts with the goals of other nations. Each nation's pride caused them to exaggerate disputes with other countries. In addition, several countries, who had become independent from the Ottoman empire, wanted control over the Balkan States, known as the "Powder Keg of Europe." Many countries also became involved in disputes over their boundaries.

The rise of nationalism encouraged countries to build-up their military might for protection against other countries. Germany began this build-up and other countries followed its lead. Technological advances enabled countries to develop more sophisticated weapons and to quickly ship them to where they were needed most.

The competition for colonies in Asia and Africa was great during the late 1800s and early 1900s. The industrialization of European countries created a need for supplies and raw materials, which could be found in the colonized countries. This competition for colonies strained relations among the European countries.

Many countries formed alliances with other countries. The alliances required one country to help protect other countries in the alliance. It provided a sense of security. However, alliances required a country to go to war even if it had no personal quarrel with another country. The Triple

Alliance consisting of Germany, Italy, and Austria-Hungary was such an alliance.

[Summary]

In summary, the conditions that caused the outbreak of the first World War were the rise of nationalism, the build-up of military power, competition for colonies, and military alliances between the European countries.

Write Neatly And Legibly

Be conscious of your writing, and write as neatly and legibly as humanly possible. Print if necessary. It may take a little more time, but it may spell the difference between the grader understanding and not understanding your essay.

Check Your Grammar, Spelling And Punctuation

Always check your paper for proper spelling, grammar and punctuation. Demonstrate that in addition to knowing the material, you can effectively communicate it.

Use Pencil:
Write On Every Other Line

Unless required to do otherwise, always write in *pencil* and write on *every other line*. There are several good reasons for doing this.

First, with a good eraser in hand (remember your MAGIC RUB), you can completely erase a word or sentence without having your paper look as if it went through a washing machine. Second, writing on every other line gives your essay a clean appearance.  It also makes your writing easier to read because the tails from the letters on the line above do not interfere with the words below. Third, you can insert words cleanly on the skipped lines. Remember, your paper just might be the last one the grader sees after a tough evening of grading messy papers.

Review the sample essays shown in Exhibits 10.4 and 10.5. Notice how the essay in Exhibit 10.4 appears sloppy. It is difficult to follow because of the numerous places where text is inserted. In contrast, Exhibit 10.5 is easy to read and follow. Even though some information was added, it does not detract from the overall appearance of this essay.

Essay Answer

~~Nationalism was a strong so~~ The 4 basic causes for the outbreak of world War I were nationalism, military build-up, competition for colonies in Asia & Africa, and alliances between the countries.

Each nation's plan caused them to explore and dispute with other sea nations.

Nationalism was a strong sense of loyalty to a ~~confi countries~~ country's political, *economic* goals. This was an extreme sense of patriotism that caused conflicts with the goals of other nations. In addition, several countries, who had become independent from the Ottoman Empire, wanted control over the Balkan States.

Exhibit 10.4

Essay Answer

The four basic causes for the outbreak of World

War I were: nationalism, military build-ups,

competition for colonies in Asia and Africa, and

military alliances between the countries.

Nationalism was a strong ~~stat~~ sense of loyalty
                                    and economic
to a country's political, goals. This was an

extreme sense of patriotism that caused

conflicts with the goals of other nations. Each
nation's pride caused them to exaggerate disputes w/ other countries.
In addition, several countries, who had become

independent from the Ottoman Empire, wanted

control over the Balkan States, known as the

"Powder Keg of Europe." Many countries also

became involved in disputes over their boundaries.

Exhibit 10.5

TRUE/FALSE EXAMS

With true/false exams you can apply many of the skills and strategies you learned for multiple choice exams. Always underline or highlight the keywords, especially when a *not* is included in the question. Read each question carefully.

As with multiple-choice questions, be particularly alert for those questions containing absolutes. Absolutes are words such as *all*, *every*, *never* or *none*. When you see an absolute in a question, the entire question or statement must be true, if not, the statement is false. Questions that contain absolutes are often false. For example consider the statement, *All the southern states seceded from the Union simultaneously.*

You know that all the southern states did secede from the Union and formed the Confederate States of America. This part of the statement is therefore true. However, the statement also says the states seceded simultaneously. This is not true because South Carolina seceded first and was joined later by the other southern states. The entire statement is therefore false.

Guessing on true/false exams is easier than guessing on multiple choice exams. On a true/false exam, you have a one in two chance of guessing the correct answer. With multiple choice, you have to work up to these odds. When you have *no choice* but to guess on a true/false exam, guess true because (1) more correct responses tend to be true, and (2) teachers find it more difficult to make up a false statement than a true one.

SHORT ANSWER EXAMS

Short answer exams can require you to fill in a blank or provide an answer in the form of one or more sentences. *Think* before you rush to answer the question. When you cannot think of an answer immediately, jot down a few keywords or ideas and consider the question for a minute or so. If you cannot decide on an answer, go on and return to the question later.

Write clearly and legibly. Print if you think you should. Do your best to answer every question!

Review the following sample short answer question.

SAMPLE QUESTION[3]

QUESTION:

Define ozone and describe its function in the earth's atmosphere.

SUGGESTED KEYWORDS/PHRASES:

Form of oxygen; three oxygen atoms; O_3; absorbs UV radiation; filters out UV radiation; 19-20 miles.

SUGGESTED ANSWER:

Ozone is a form of oxygen that exists in the earth's atmosphere. Its molecules each contain three oxygen atoms. Its symbol is O_3. The highest concentration of ozone exists in the atmosphere at a height of about 19 miles. It effectively filters the sun's dangerous ultraviolet radiation and keeps this radiation from reaching earth.

MATCHING EXAMS

In a matching exam, you are given two lists of items. You must relate an item in one list with an item in the other. Sometimes each list will have the same number of items. At other times, one list will have more items than the other.

Matching exams can be confusing if you do not approach them in a systematic way. Start with the longer list (if one is longer) and cover all items but the first one. This will focus your attention on this item only. Then, search the opposite column for the correct match. When you select the proper match, cross out the items in both lists. Crossing out your selection will prevent you from considering the item again when looking for another match. Next, go to item two in the list of covered items and repeat the same sequence of steps as for item one. Consider the following example to illustrate the process.

Match the items in column one with the proper dates in column two:

I	II
1. Civil War ends	a. 1732
2. Revolutionary War ends	b. 1863
3. America's independence	c. 1865
4. George Washington born	d. 1776
5. Battle of Gettysburg	e. 1783

In this example you can begin with either column. Assume you decide to start with column I. Cover choices 2 through 5. Now, consider only 1, Civil War ends. Search column II until you find the correct answer, which is *c*, 1865. Cross out 1 in column I and *c* in column II.

Next, consider 2 in column I, Revolutionary War ends. Cover the remaining items in column I, 3 through 5. Now search column II for the correct answer, which is *e*, 1783. Cross out 2 in column I and *e* in column II. Finish the matching exercise following the same sequence of steps.

A matching exam can be completed more quickly when you approach it in the systematic fashion described above. This technique is effective because you consider possible choices only once instead of several times.

Summary

Plan to get a good night's sleep before an exam. You will perform at your best when you are rested. Eat and drink sensibly before an exam. Too much food can make you sleepy and too much drink can increase trips to the rest room, disrupting your concentration.

Prepare a checklist of the items you must have and review this list before leaving for the exam. If one is required, make sure *admission slip* is at the top of your list. Arrive early. The peace of mind will be worth the few extra minutes waiting.

Get into a positive frame of mind. Use the time before the exam to build your confidence. Avoid listening to the idle chatter of students quizzing each other outside the exam room. You are prepared and ready.

Sit as close to the front of the room as possible. From this seat, you can see the examiner and hear all specific instructions. If you feel anxious before or during the exam, take a few deep breaths. Deep breathing has a relaxing effect. If necessary, close your eyes for a few minutes.

Listen to all instructions and read all directions. Failure to do so could have disastrous consequences. Take a few minutes to survey the exam. You will see how much you do know and your confidence will be boosted. Allocate your time properly. You must finish the entire exam.

Thoroughly read all questions. Underline all keywords. It is easy to misinterpret a question if you do not see keywords such as *not* or *all*. Work at your own pace. Do not rush to leave because others have finished first.

During the exam, maintain faith and confidence in yourself. Recall your past exam successes. Ensure that all your test papers are neat and have a pleasing appearance. A neat paper is more likely to receive the maximum points available.

Answer every question on the exam. You must provide an answer to receive at least partial credit. Draw a diagram if you are having difficulty understanding a question. Diagrams enable you to solve a problem *visually*, which is a powerful tool.

During the exam, try to visualize your notes or your 3x5 cards. This mental picture of your notes will help you to recall. Recall can be aided further by imagining the conditions under which you learned the material, for example, the temperature or smell of the room.

Check your answers for common sense. Do not rush to complete a question without giving thought as to its reasonableness.

After you finish, forget the exam until you receive your grade. You cannot change the results. Learn from your exams. Review your wrong answers and decide why the answers are not correct. You also must understand what types of questions the instructor may ask and how the instructor expects you to respond.

Try to answer multiple choice questions without looking at the answers. Highlight or underline all keywords and *do not rush* to select the first answer that appears correct. Try to evaluate each possible answer as if it were a true or false question. Record your answers in the answer book and on the answer sheet. Pay particular attention to the form and layout of the answer sheet. Finally, review your answers and do not change an answer unless you are absolutely sure your first response was incorrect.

When answering essay questions, think before writing and prepare an outline of your answer. Use pencil, if permitted, and write on every other line to keep a neat and pleasing appearance. When finished, review your answer and check it for proper spelling, grammar, and punctuation.

In a true/false exam, highlight or underline the keywords and especially note words such as *all*, *every*, *never* or *none*. When you see one of these words, the *entire* question or statement must be true, if not, the statement is false.

Short answer exams can require you to fill in a blank or provide an answer in the form of one or more sentences. *Think* before you rush to answer a question, and write legibly.

When taking a matching exam, start with the first item of one list and cover up the remaining answers in that list. As you select an answer from the opposite list, cross-out the matching answers. This process provides a systematic way to answer the questions, and prevents you from considering the same answer twice.

The ladder of success is never crowded at the top.

Napoleon Hill

Chapter Twelve

AFTERWORD:

MAINTAINING YOUR ACHIEVEMENT

Learn to be The Master Student has exposed you to the wonders of discovering and developing your potential. You have also been given some ideas and tools to begin the job. It is now up to you act on what you have learned and to *continue* learning from other people and sources of information. Learn from your parents, teachers, co-workers, friends and other books that can further your development.

To make effective use of the information presented, you must practice the techniques and skills presented in this book. You must practice them until they become a part of you, until they become a habit. Most importantly, maintain your new level of achievement, maintain a positive *can do* attitude. Believe in yourself.

After winning seven football games in a row, a member of the Washington Redskins described the team's success to the Washington Post.

> *"I'm numb about what's going on with this team,"
> running back Earnest Byner said. "I've never
> been associated with something like this. I've
> been on good teams, championship teams, but
> never a team going like this. We're to the point
> where we go out and expect to win. We know we
> still have to take care of business, but we do
> expect to win. That's a good feeling."*

This is the attitude of the master athlete, the master team, and it carried the Redskins to a Super Bowl victory. It is also the attitude of *The Master Student*. You must *expect* the best.

In addressing a group of fifth graders before sending them on to middle school, Dr. Thomas Poore, a Maryland elementary school principal, admonished his students to (1) fervently pursue any goal they set for themselves, and (2) not allow any person or test score to keep them from their goal. He told the students that with dedication and hard work, they could reach any goal they desire.

Dr. Poore's advice to his students and Earnest Byner's assessment of the Redskins' success summarize effectively the important message being presented in *Learn to be The Master Student*. That is, with a firm belief in yourself and determination to reach your goals, you can achieve anything you desire. Learn to become your own best friend: not your worst enemy.

ENDNOTES

1. Webster's Encyclopedic Dictionary of the English Language, New York: Lexicon Publications, Inc. (1989), p. 988.

2. The 1988 Edition of the World Book Encyclopedia was used as the reference source for this example.

3. The 1988 Edition of the World Book Encyclopedia was used as the reference source for this example.

RESOURCES/BIBLIOGRAPHY

Books

The following books cover the subjects of self-image, personal development, positive thinking, memory, and study skills. Most, if not all, are available at your public library.

One book is quite different from the rest, but its message is powerful just the same. *Getting Well Again* discusses the successes researchers have had in getting cancer patients to use the power of their minds to help rid their bodies of cancer. In particular, the patients are taught to use *relaxation and visualization* techniques to assist in their cure.

Allen, James. *As a Man Thinketh.* Peter Pauper Press, Inc.: New York.

Blanchard, Kenneth and Johnson, Spencer. *The One Minute Manager.* Berkley Books: New York, 1982.

Buzan, Tony. *Use Both Sides Of Your Brain.* E. P. Dutton: New York, 1983.

Carnegie, Dale. *The Quick And Easy Way To Effective Public Speaking.* Dale Carnegie and Associates: New York, 1962.

Colligan, Louise. *Scholastics A+ Guide To Taking Tests.* Scholastics, Inc.: New York, 1982.

Ehrenberg, Miriam. *Optimum Brain Power.* Dodd, Mead, and Co: New York, 1985.

Feder, Bernard. *The Complete Guide To Taking Tests.* Prentice-Hall: Englewood Cliffs, New Jersey, 1979.

Felleman, Hazel. *The Best Loved Poems of the American People.* Doubleday: New York, 1936.

Ferraro, Susan. *Remembrance Of Things Fast.* Laurel Books: New York, 1990.

Fry, Ronald. *How To Study*. The Career Press: Hawthorne, New Jersey, 1989.

Garland, John. *Muscling The Multiple Choice*. TW Concepts: Middletown, Pennsylvania, 1989.

Higbee, Kenneth L. *Your Memory: How It Works And How To Improve It*. Prentice Hall Press: New York, 1988.

Hill, Napoleon. *Think And Grow Rich*. Fawcett Crest: New York, 1960.

Johnson, Spencer. *One Minute For Myself*. Avon Books: New York, 1987.

Johnson, Spencer and Johnson, Constance. *The One Minute Teacher*. William Morrow and Co.: New York, 1986.

Lorayne, Harry. *Super Memory/Super Student*. Little, Brown and Company: Boston, 1990.

Maltz, Maxwell. *Psycho-Cybernetics*. Willshire Book Company: Hollywood, 1960.

Minninger, Joan. *Total Recall*. Rodale Press: Emmaus, Pa., 1984.

Perry, Susan and Dawson, Jim. *The Secrets Our Body Clocks Reveal*. Ballantine Books: New York 1988.

Rowntree, Derek. *Learn How To Study*. Scribner's: New York, 1984.

Schafer, Edith Nalle. *Our Remarkable Memory*. Starhill Press: Washington, DC, 1988.

Schutz, Susan Polis. *Don't Ever Give Up Your Dreams*. Blue Mountain Press: Boulder Colorado, 1983.

Simonton, O. Carl; Matthews-Simonton, Stephanie; Creighton, James L. *Getting Well Again*. Bantam Books, New York, 1988.

Suplee, Curt. *Memory*. The Washington Post Magazine. Washington, D.C., October 7, 1990

Von Oech, Roger. *A Whack On The Side Of The Head*. Warner Books: New York, 1983.

--------------. *What Works: Research About Teaching And Learning.* United States Department of Education, 1987.

Books for Elementary School Students

Author Marilyn Berry has written an excellent series of study guides, complete with illustrations to make the guides easily understandable by children. The authors highly recommend these books, which are:

Help Is On the Way For: Book Reports. Children's Press: Chicago, 1984.

Help Is On the Way For: Charts and Graphs. Children's Press: Chicago, 1985.

Help Is On the Way For: Group Reports. Children's Press: Chicago, 1985.

Help Is On the Way For: Listening Skills. Children's Press: Chicago, 1986.

Help Is On the Way For: Math Skills. Children's Press: Chicago, 1985.

Help Is On the Way For: Memory Skills. Children's Press: Chicago, 1985.

Help Is On the Way For: Outlining Skills. Children's Press: Chicago, 1985.

Help Is On the Way For: Spelling Skills. Children's Press: Chicago, 1985.

Help Is On the Way For: Thinking Skills. Children's Press: Chicago, 1986.

Help Is On the Way For: Written Reports. Children's Press: Chicago, 1984.

Audio Tape Programs

Nightingale, Earl. *Lead The Field*. Nightingale-Conant
      Corporation: Chicago.
Peale, Dr. Norman Vincent. *The Power of Positive Thinking*.
      Simon and Schuster: New York, 1987.
Robbins, Anthony. *Personal Power*. Guthy-Renker
      Corporation: Irwindale, California, 1989.
Stone, W. Clement and Hill, Napoleon. *Success Through A
      Positive Mental Attitude*. Nightingale-Conant
      Corporation: Chicago.

INDEX

A

B

C

D

229

Y

Scholarship Offer

To demonstrate our commitment to student achievement, Maydale Publishing will use 5% of our profits to award $500 scholarships. We will award a least two scholarships each year, regardless of profits. To apply to win a $500 scholarship, send your name, address, telephone number, and grade or college level. Send this information to Maydale Publishing, Scholarship Offer, P. O. Box 10359, Silver Spring, MD 20914. Include a paragraph addressing each of the following:

1. Why you need this scholarship.

2. How your confidence level has affected your performance.

3. Your goals and how you plan to achieve them.

4. The study techniques you believe to be most effective, and why you believe they are effective. These techniques may be original or some of those presented in this book.

We will be the sole judge of winning entries. Each entry will be judged on originality, content, and clarity. All submissions become the property of Maydale Publishing Company, Inc. We reserve the right to use any submissions in our newsletter or a revised copy of *Learn to be The Master Student*. We will pay $25.00 for any entry, or portion thereof, used in any subsequent publication. **You do not have to purchase a copy of this book or any other product to be eligible.**

NOTES

NOTES

ORDER FORM

Telephone orders: Call Toll Free: 1-800-247-6553. Have your VISA or MasterCard ready.

*Fax Orders: 1-419-281-6883

Postal Orders: Maydale Publishing Company, Inc., P.O. Box 10359, Silver Spring, MD 20914

Please send ___ copies of Learn to be The Master Student @ $14.95 per copy. I understand that I may return any books for a full refund, no questions asked.

☐ **Please send a complimentary copy of *The Master Student Newsletter*.**

Name: _____

Address: _____

City: _____ **State:** _____ **Zip:** _____-_____

Sales tax:
Maryland and Ohio residents please add 5% sales tax.

Shipping:
Book rate: $2.00 for each book.
(Surface Shipping may take three to four weeks)
First class: $3.50 per book

Payment:

☐ Check

☐ VISA

☐ MasterCard

Card number: _____**Expiration date:** _____

Name on card: _____

240